Dream Catcher 41

Stairwell Books //

Dream Catcher 41

**Editor Emeritus
And Founder**
Paul Sutherland

Editor
Amina Alyal

Editorial Board
John Gilham (Retired Editor)
Tanya Parker Nightingale
Pauline Kirk
Rose Drew
Alan Gillott
Clint Wastling
Greg McGee

Art Advisor
Greg McGee

Production Managers
Alan Gillott and Rose Drew

Subscriptions to Dream Catcher Magazine

£15.00 UK (Two issues inc. p&p)
£22.00 Europe
£25.00 USA and Canada

Cheques should be made
payable to **Dream Catcher**
and sent to:

Dream Catcher Subscriptions

161 Lowther Street

York, YO31 7LZ

UK

+44 1904 733767

argillott@gmail.com

www.dreamcatchermagazine.co.uk
@literaryartsmag
www.stairwellbooks.co.uk
@stairwellbooks

Dream Catcher Magazine

Dream Catcher No. 41

ISSN: 1466-9455

Published by Stairwell Books //

ISBN: 978-1-913432-05-8

York UNESCO
City of Media Arts   YORK

Contents – Authors

FEATURED ARTIST

Surrounded in childhood by Classical Composer portraits and discussions of Constable, the first Christmas of Jeffrey Spedding's teenage years came accompanied with an oil painting set. The gift fell on fertile ground and the young Jeffrey soon harnessed oil paint's glossy viscosity. It must have been no small achievement for a teenager in the 1950s, for with considerable rigour and alacrity Jeffrey Spedding studied at Wimbledon School of Art after leaving school, taught at Swansea Institute of Higher Education, and progressed upwards in all things pedagogical until he held the position of Associate Dean of School of the Arts at Northampton University.

All this time, and beyond, like all artists should, Jeffery painted every day. It is this striving for personal excellence in his chosen genre that sets Spedding's personal oeuvre apart. It is the eventual blossoming of his chosen tools that inculcate a yearning for pure visual attainment: the interfusion of oil, acrylic, emulsion is no accident, nor is it a short cut into mere painterly energy. Spedding saw in the world around him a relentless barrage of formal relationships that he was compelled to catch, like lightning in a bottle, and if it meant painting every day, teasing the tensions between dry and matt water-based paint and the ooze of oil (try it!), skewering the shifting shapes of nature with careful photography for subsequent transitions into mixed media painting, then so be it. What Jeffery Spedding called 'Compositional Activity' became a priority, and his output increased as he perfected his technique.

It was classical music that helped kickstart a thirteen year old Jeffery's confidence in painting, and it was classical music that continued to provide the conceptual structure of his maverick approach. He was aware of how Rembrandt and Turner saw similar synergies between melody and painting – that a composer's material is best when it blossoms – and how a painter can develop the depiction and descriptive stage to engender a radical and previously unimagined quality, that which I can only describe as a quickening, or the pulse of a painting. Jefferey Spedding must have gained great satisfaction in seeing his art attain similar, transformative power.

He continued to nurture the symbiosis of classical music and his individual compositional activity. His art became highly regarded, and was exhibited in London's Royal Festival Hall, Cardiff's St David's Hall, Cork Street's Richmond Gallery, amongst others. Permanent displays in public venues popped up all the UK, with Edward Greenfield, chief music critic of The Guardian, championing his art and becoming an avid collector.

In terms of compositions, his subject matter moved increasingly towards the landscape of the UK and France. His creative existence with author Sally Spedding was obviously idyllic and contributed to his progressive practice: "We built a bolt hole in the Pyrénées-Orientales. I am particularly interested in uninhabited fields with trees. My main influence here is the music of Debussy, and his use of open, whole tones. My painting as a result, has become more concerned with the fleeting movement of blocks or passages of form rather than more focused elements." It is here that as avid followers of painting we witness Spedding enter a crucial phase of depicting the world around him with unique, energetic mark making, bringing it to life with idiosyncratic flair.

Sadly, the suddenness of death plays a part in this story. Jeff Spedding died suddenly, like his Dad who bought him his oil paint set all those years ago, from a ruptured aorta, in February 2019. He is survived by his wife Sally. His painting, in its bristling restlessness, continues to bring balm and boosted spirits to all who have their lives enhanced by Art, Music, and indeed Poetry.

Greg McGee, June 2020

PAGES OF ARTWORK

We are grateful to Jeffrey's widow, Sally, for permission to feature her late husband's work in Dream Catcher. Sally has also contributed a review of David J. Costello's book, *Heft.*

Putting together Dream Catcher 41 in lockdown has been a multi-layered experience. Not only did the practicalities of adjusting to the new normal delay production somewhat, but the vast majority of the pieces were written before the pandemic, which descended on us with such unexpected haste. Only a few were written during it. But reading them all through the lens of the new normal casts a different colour on the pieces and their themes – isolation, for example, masks, nature's forces. They are preoccupied with thoughts we are slowly returning to, having been overwhelmed by the cultural, individual and tragic impacts of the pandemic, reminding us of the issues humanity still has to engage with, now alongside the added dimension of virus control. So global pollution, homelessness, xenophobia, race, political ideologies – all still need our attention. We are still, perhaps more poignantly than ever, interested in our personal pasts, in hospitals and mortality, in the borderlands between urban and rural life.

Literary life in lockdown has been in some ways surprisingly rich, thanks to online communication and the festivals, open mics, readings, book launches, writing groups, and theatre productions readily available to a wider audience than ever before, and the furloughed time for many to engage with them. For some, such activities are more accessible than they were. And while we have been physically restricted to our own immediate neighbourhood, we have been coming together virtually across national and international distances in ways that are simply impractical in real life. Isolation combined with intensified virtual conversation has undoubtedly had a bearing on the searching, iconoclastic development of the Black Lives Matter movement. Reading and local walking have flourished, with many going on their own regular *derive*, foraging, observing, thinking. And contemplating this issue of Dream Catcher while engaging with such an altered and heightened mindfulness draws fresh perspectives out of the pieces, and new ironies. We are, perhaps, in the process of generating a distinctive 'interpretive community', in the phrase made popular by Stanley Fish, so that our own reader response is shifting with the accelerated shift of our globally shared, historical moment.

The writers in this issue write movingly, cleverly, musically, and amusingly, about loneliness, memories of childhood, romance and disillusioned romance, quotidian life in urban contexts, gardens, family relationships, in memoriam and in different global locations. There are witty stories, reflective, interiorised poems, poems that ponder literature itself, and the spiritual and mythic archetypes that inform our consciousnesses.

Amina Alyal

23rd December 2018

Dear Peter,

It's that time of year again – the moment my annual newsletter lands on your doormat. And how the year has flown. Such a shame we didn't manage a get-together – next year for sure!

January in Bayston Bridge was biting – was it where you are? We had snow here for five whole days and there was a terrible collision on the main road when a lorry skidded on the ice and ran into a row of parked cars. Perhaps you saw it on the news? After that, the council finally agreed to grit more regularly. The event was covered by the local papers for at least a week.

Spring sprung, as they say, and I shall skip to the summer. Don't worry – I'm not going to chronicle every week of the year. As you know, I'm not one of those pedantic newsletter writers – just the highlights!

And so, onto August and my summer holiday in Whitby. Originally, I had planned to do some beach walking and visit the abbey with a friend of mine, Joanne – I may have mentioned her in my last letter – but unfortunately she had made alternative holiday plans with a girlfriend of hers. However, it was an extremely pleasant trip and I would thoroughly recommend Whitby Abbey gift shop if ever you find yourself in that part of the world.

September welcomed a fine harvest of apples. You may remember my complaining the previous year of a very poor crop. Well, no slim pickings this time. Twelve apples and not one of them infested or rotten. It pays to keep a close eye, let me tell you. They lasted a number of weeks - it was well worth the hours spent monitoring the tree at the kitchen window.

And now we come to the Christmas month. I was sorry not to be able to invite you and the family here to share in the festivities, but unfortunately I am rather short on space and, as I've explained before, I have nowhere to put the children (and they're rather large now aren't they? Fifteen and seventeen, is that right?), or Rachel for that matter. I could hardly expect you to come without your own wife, despite the many Christmases we cousins spent together as children. I am rather easier to accommodate I expect, being only one, but people do get very busy and 'booked up', as they say, around Christmas time. No matter.

I am too late for the post now so I expect this will reach you after Christmas. Therefore, let me wish you a belated Merry Christmas. Perhaps you could write in the new year with some suggested dates for a meet-up?

All the best,

George

Dear Peter,

Firstly, let me reassure you – I haven't gone mad! I know it's not my turn to write, but I have a spare afternoon so I thought I'd get you up to speed with events in Bayston Bridge.

April is such a lively time of year, don't you think? The world has emerged from hibernation and there's so much to see, even on one's own modest patch of lawn. Although, I remind myself, it's not my patch of lawn, as such, but the landlord's. He's very good though – hardly ever bothers me. In fact, I don't think I've seen him once since I moved in four years ago. I don't suppose he feels the need, seeing as I always pay my rent on time. I'm a model tenant!

Anyhow, now that the year is well-established, as they say, I was wondering if you'd had any thoughts about dates. I know, it's easier for me being single – I don't have all those family commitments and social engagements like you do – but I was hoping we might be able to pencil something in soon? After all, we're both retired now so it shouldn't be too difficult.

Let me know. Looking forward to hearing from you.

All the best,

George

31st May 2019

Dear Peter,

Thought I'd drop you a line to let you know my change of address – please see top of page. Hopefully, you haven't sent a letter in the past couple of days – I'm afraid it might not reach me if so.

As you can see, I'm no longer in Bayston Bridge, but thankfully I managed to secure a lovely flat in the larger, neighbouring town of Dunthorp. It's not as picturesque as the village, of course, but I only have to walk to the next street to be at the riverside, which is an unexpected bonus.

Perhaps I ought to explain the sudden change. It's quite simple – my landlord decided to retire. I hadn't realised he was fifty-five – everyone looks so young to me! The sale of the house was necessary in order to achieve this and so naturally I had to move. Apparently he has a commercial buyer – one of these supermarket 'express' shops is looking to convert the whole row. Anyway, he gave me two weeks, which wasn't quite long enough for me to sort my things out and unfortunately I couldn't remove all my belongings before the eviction process kicked in. I wasn't aware that landlords are allowed to keep your belongings if you leave them behind, even for a day. No matter, the flat isn't quite as big as the old place, and I don't think I could have squeezed my kitchen table into the lift! I'm sorry about my box of Dad's old theatre programmes though, and my collection of cassette tapes. Oh, I know I can't play them anymore, but they were nice to have. Reminded me of our mothers dancing round the living room at family get-togethers – do you remember? Poetry in Motion, Blue Moon, Walkin' Back to Happiness, all the oldies.

Tomorrow, I'm hoping to drop in on the landlord and ask for my belongings back. He has a house in the village too, so I know where to find him. I don't much mind about the furniture – as I say, I have a lot less room now – but those collections have real sentimental value. I'm sure he'll be glad to have them off his hands. I'll have to hire a taxi to transport the boxes I suppose. Oh, I'm rambling now so I'll sign off – only intended to notify you of my new circumstances.

All the best,
George

8th June 2019

Dear Peter,

I'm sorry that this letter comes hot on the heels of my previous note, but I really do need another person's opinion on my situation. It is regarding my collections – you know, my Beano magazines dating back to when we were boys in the 60s; my cotton spools – I have some real treasures in there: Clark's Mile End Spool Cotton, Barbour's Linen Thread, Chadwick's Six Cord, Dewhurst Sylko; several hundred Bryant and May matchboxes. Not to mention the cassettes and theatre programmes. I could go on – I had hired a people carrier taxi in anticipation of picking them all up from the landlord's residence. However, when I got there, his wife informed me that he'd taken everything to the tip a couple of days previously. Apparently, he had assumed it was all rubbish that I'd left behind to be spiteful. She then went on to say that I should receive a bill shortly to cover the cost of the removal of said 'rubbish'. I took the taxi onwards to the tip and rummaged as deeply as I could, but couldn't find a single cotton spool. Everything in there was soaked anyway – we've had a lot of early summer showers recently. One of the officials in a high-vis told me I was breaking the law by leaning into the skip so I reluctantly gave up and came back to the flat. I am really at a loss as to what to do. How can I ever get my collections back? Oh, Peter, why did this have to happen? What shall I do?

All the best,
George

31st July 2019

Dear Peter,

Firstly, I must apologise to you. I fear my last letter will have worried you a great deal. I wrote it in haste – I was in a bit of a state, I must admit – and I didn't stop to think about how you might feel reading it. Let me reassure you now that I am quite well again and back to my old self. For a few days, my world seemed to collapse in on itself, but, you'll be glad to hear, I've dragged myself out of that hole and I'm determined to use the experience as a springboard into a more positive future. Yes, I lost my collections, some of which were very dear to me, and yes, I went back to the landlord and stood at the corner of his road, building up the courage to give him a piece of my mind (you'll be relieved to hear I decided against it and went back to the flat without embarrassing myself). But losing my most precious possessions, items I've held on to all these years, has made me look at other objects with a new eye. Suddenly, the most banal of items has gained an unexpected value. Pigeon feathers, for example. Have you ever looked at a pigeon's wing feather up close? It is quite beautiful I assure you. And a number of them together can be quite extraordinary – a piece of art! Other collections are more useful – if you ever need a spare part for a vacuum cleaner, I'll be able to sort you out. Some items take up less space: I have at least thirty cable ties now, and that's only after a month of collecting!

As you can see, I'm quite recovered and perhaps, I might venture, even happier than before. I have more collections than ever. The flat is smaller than my old house and my kaleidoscope of treasure does take up rather a lot of space, but I can still live quite comfortably here.

Anyway, the intention of this letter was to reassure you and I hope it has achieved its aim. Therefore, now that I'm back on track, I wonder if we can get back to arranging a day to meet? I haven't heard from you for a while. Are you still there? Ha, just joking. Write soon!

All the best,
George

25th November 2019
Dear Peter,

As you can see, this year I have thought ahead and am superseding my usual annual newsletter to write to you well before Christmas to give us time enough to organise a visit. I thought perhaps I could pop in between Christmas and the new year? I don't know about you, and I might have this completely wrong – I admit, I have little experience of trying to shuffle a whole family around during the festive period – but the week between Christmas and the new year is often rather subdued and quiet for me.

Don't worry, when I say 'pop by', I really do mean a flying visit as I plan to be on the Wirral for a few days anyway - I've always fancied a wintry beach walk and I've heard there's a wonderful selection of soaps at the Port Sunlight gift shop: I've sorted out quite a little holiday for myself. As I was putting it together, I suddenly thought, Why don't I pop in to see Peter whilst I'm there? And the family of course, Rachel, and the children. How does the Thursday sound? Or the Wednesday or Friday – I'm pretty flexible (the museum is open every day except New Year's Day). Anyway,

I have your address, so I could simply drop in – let me know when you'll be around.

I have a wonderful little collection to give you – I don't mind parting with this one; it's a collection I've been putting together for a few weeks with you in mind. I don't think I'm letting the cat out of the bag by admitting you might already have one of these, but a group of five is so much more satisfying. Very helpful if you happen to lose one. Or two. Or if you like a variety of colours. Right, enough, or I'll spoil the surprise!

See you soon and all the best,

George

5th January 2020

Dear Peter,

I'm writing in lieu of wishing you a Merry Christmas and a Happy New Year in person. I'm still trying to understand how I missed you. Perhaps you were away for the entire festive period? If that is the case, I must say, I wish you'd let me know. I tried your house at least four times over the three days I was there, and once the lights were on, so I have to assume you were around. Or perhaps a neighbour popped in to feed the cat? Do you have a cat? In the end, I had to leave your present in the shed round the side of the house – I hope you don't mind my going in there, but the wrapping paper would have got soggy in all the rain if I'd left the package on the doorstep. Not that the collection itself would have been much damaged: all spatulas are made of rubber these days.

Anyway, after my Wirral holiday, I'm back in my flat amongst all my things, which, I must admit, is rather comforting. The stacks are forever growing, but there is not one collection I'd go without. You simply don't know when you might need a 30-centimetre ruler or a light fitting or a plastic bag. And the local newspapers are full of useful information if ever you want to reference back to, say, summer 2019 in Bayston Bridge.

Unfortunately, the new landlord is rather more intrusive than my previous one and, despite his unkindness at the end of my tenancy, at least the last one allowed me my privacy. This new one, 'Clive,' seems to be forever on my doorstep, peering over my shoulder and frowning. His suggestion of 'hoarding' yesterday quite got my back up. He is, of course, rather ignorant, but that does not excuse his ill-mannered attitude.

Oh, I don't mean to grumble, and I am glad to be back in Dunthorp. The great joy of a holiday is returning home, don't you think? That's enough for now. I'll wait to hear from you.

All the best,

George

25th January 2020

Dear Peter,

The best laid plans o' Mice an' Men gang aft agley. There – I just had to write it down. Ever since they played a reading of the Robbie Burns' poem on the radio this morning, I've had this particular line rattling around my head - I simply had to get it out and I'm afraid you're the unfortunate recipient. It's a pertinent point though, don't you think? Sometimes, I look around my little flat and wonder how I got here.

Remember the plans we had when we were boys? We were going to go to the moon or drive steam trains across the country or be a famous singing duo. Do you remember the little performances we did for our mothers? I wish I had photos of those outfits we would put together from the dressing-up box. I'm sure you used to hog the purple feather boa! Yes, we had great ambitions for our futures – we always said we'd do these things together. Life happens though, doesn't it, and various forces pull us apart. I'm sure it's all for the best; I know you must be very happy with Rachel and the children. Still, we have the future to look forward to and, as the great Scottish poet said, 'An' forward though I canna see…' Well, I can't remember the part after that.

'Clive' has been around again. At least, I'm assuming it's him banging on the door and shouting through the letterbox. Fortunately, I have built a number of stacks and piles of collections in the entrance hall to obscure his vision when he peers through the letterbox flap to see if I'm in. Sometimes, I have to wait hours inside before it's safe to come out. It's at times like these I really do appreciate my little transistor radio I picked up from a wheelie bin outside my block of flats. I couldn't believe my luck! I suppose they're becoming obsolete what with all this new technology around, but I can certainly make use of it. Anyway, I managed to listen right through from Start the Week to the end of The World At One yesterday before emerging from my flat for a loaf of bread to make a sandwich. There was a note stuck to my door, but I just put it with my collection of headed notepaper documents – did I tell you about the letter written on Harrods notepaper? Someone in my building has fancy connections – and popped out for a bit of shopping.

Actually, I've had the little radio playing almost constantly since I plucked it from the bin of oblivion, and I find it hard to drag myself away – there are so many wonderful programmes. In the end of course, I do take myself out – I'll suddenly worry I haven't enough of this, that or the other, and I do always return from a treasure hunt with piles of useful items, not to mention batteries to keep the radio going – but I don't like to miss too much whilst I'm away.

I suppose I'm telling you about my radio because I don't want you to worry, Peter. I know I've harped on at times about arranging a date to meet up, but I understand how difficult it must be for you to make time. Anyway, I want you to know that I'm fine.

All the best,
George

Dear Peter,

Just a short note, my friend. As you can see, I haven't written a return address at the top. The truth is, I'm unsure of where I'm headed. I am currently sitting in Dunthorp library with nothing but the contents of my rucksack: my leather coin pouch with my bus pass in, my glasses case, and a few treasures I picked up this morning (an ivory photo frame with curlicues in the corners, three matching coasters with a wintry Christmas design, and the lid of a reusable bamboo coffee cup – it's amazing what people will throw away. Oh, and yesterday's Herald of course – I haven't missed a single issue since last June). I have borrowed this writing paper and pen from the kindly librarian.

After my treasure-seeking this morning, I went back to the flat for a spot of lunch. Imagine my surprise when my key wouldn't work in the lock. I tried for several minutes, but to no avail. In the end, a woman I've never seen before but assume to be my neighbour, came down from the flat upstairs to say the landlord had had someone in that morning to change the locks. I must have stared at her, mouth agape, because she then went on to say I'd had enough warnings and the state of my flat was a disgrace and a fire hazard to us all. I wasn't sure who she meant by 'us' but I suddenly felt the full force of being locked out. My little transistor radio is still in there.

I have a pleasant view at this library window – the river passes right underneath it – but the rain has just started to come down and the trees in the park are being battered a little by the winds. A weather feature in yesterday's paper said February is officially the wettest month of the year. Mind you, the lights in the café windows are pretty through the rain, don't you think, especially the red and pink ones. Of course, I hadn't realised it's all due to Valentine's Day. I hope they keep the lights up for a few more weeks. It would be a shame to get rid of them straight away. They make the long winter seem a little more bearable.

Anyway, I said this would only be a short note and I seem to have rambled on as usual. I don't mean to go on, sorry Peter.

All the best,

George

Holly Sykes

He had been convicted of fraud to do with benefits.
They said that he was working while claiming to be unemployed.
And also claiming to be at least two people at the same time.
And if he wasn't doing that he was part of a conspiracy
so complicated it wasn't worth the trouble to untangle.
Just one look at him and you could see he was illegal.

She was thin and secretive,
looked at everyone sideways with her dark eyes.
She wore fraying tights and scuffed shoes.
She thought maybe
she only thought he was more doomed
than other people because she knew him better.

There weren't any doubts about it, however:
they had such good times together.
No one but him it seemed knew
that when she shucked off her clothes
she was like an angel from paradise.

Don't worry, he said.
He said that a lot.
He said everything was OK really.
It didn't make a big dent in her feelings
but she appreciated his mentioning his opinion.

He changed his name and dyed his hair.
Her complaint was that he was not straightforward
and not practical
and got caught.
His was that she did not respect him
and that she was so often depressed.

Gorgeous and holding roses absent-mindedly
at the midnight hour
they sail under the moon
and over the roofs of Totterdown.

Daniel Richardson

BREATHING, SHE CANNOT WARM THE AIR

I left the Royal Academy in a wrap
of eighteenth-century gentility, but clipped
along Piccadilly in contemporary haste
till a sight pulled me up sharp.

Crouched on the street is a twin
to the young Afghan on the cover of *Time*:
a woman with a rusted cavern
in the crushed velvet of her face.

The air is frosted, breathing she cannot warm it.

Hand outstretched, she begs for alms.
Do I stop to dispense cold change?
I want to get away, as she could not
when a man took up a knife, cut off her nose.

Joan Byrne

LITTLE NELL

A fix of vodka, then onto the street.
She is fighting the flashback,
pinned once again to the bitter earth
by brother and father and their acrid juice.

Here comes a punter. He cannot see her
alone up there on the cold high wire
controlling a game that can never be won.
Here in this raw colluding world
she feels like some carrier bag from a shop:
once used, that's that.

Maggie Nicholls

MID-WINTER SUNDAY

Mid-winter Sunday she lies on her back.
A warm stranger sleeps by her side,
makes her feel cold.
Night's transfusion weakens and thins.
Shadows fracture, edge into nothing.
Dawn steps out like an awkward child,
pales with waiting.

Her thoughts slide back, unwind the hours.
It is Saturday night, she sits alone.
Wind and rain hang a caul around her life.
Her brittle smile seeks comfort;
sometimes she needs warm arms against
the fall-out of this world.

He steps into her life with jazz and wine.
The wooden floor feels softer now.
She slips her shadows, holds on tight.
Her eyes are wide, a child's stare.

Mid-winter Sunday she lies on her back.
Saturday night is dead and gone.
She cannot face the ritual;
the swollen space between two strangers
feels no trace of jazz or wine on lips too dry.

She cuts loose, sheds the afterbirth of one-night stands,
opens the door as leaves pour down, black-veined in frost.
Wind drags her hair; she walks, then turns to watch
a single bird black-plumaged in the snow.
The small head tilted to the sky
awaits some song's compulsion.
She waits too ...
mid-winter Sunday, black and white.

Maggie Nicholls

It started with the shape of the letter box, putting his hand through. As if it was a mouth he had to feed. He began to think about it. How it was always dark on the other side of the door. How the letter box emitted smells and sounds and heat. Whole lives went on in there behind that dark space. The estate he delivered on was vast and impersonal. He rarely spoke to anyone, most people out, leaving notes for anything bulky – *in the garage, on the shelf, in the porch.* Or they were cautious, even afraid, behind a frosted glass front door, a drawn curtain.

It wasn't the obvious thing of a dog being on the other side with drooling jaws waiting for his fingers. (His defence would mention this, that he'd developed a phobia and that was why he did it.) The argument wasn't logical anyway because he never stopped delivering completely. Just that every day there were some he secreted, stuffed into his jacket & then transferred to the Tesco bag containing his lunch. In time he became bolder, often taking half a sack home with him, slipping it back empty the following day.

His choice of theft was random; sometimes letters so thin and slight they were almost negligible, not worth the stamp. Sometimes plump packages, bulky or squashy. Or official ones in brown envelopes, foolscap and typed.

Why he did it was mysterious even to him. Partly the secretiveness – those sealed voices, communications that he touched, had power over. He wondered, if he prised them open, what knowledge would he have of other people's lives; their thoughts, their gifts, their friendships. And the bank statements, hospital appointments, solicitor's letters, estate agent's promotions, mail order; all the random bits and pieces that formed an intricate web of information

He didn't do it for gain. He had found the odd cheque, a bank note slipped in a card. Once a cake in a purpose made box, ornate and complicated, that he ate one day in the middle of the morning. Coming home after his shift he'd pushed his way through the collapsing pile of mail to where he'd put the box and sat on the floor, tearing it open, laying hands on the moist scented concoction, gorging on the sweet spongy stuff until the cake was almost gone. Sitting there, surfeited, he'd felt something wasn't quite right, behaviour too extreme and disturbing even to him. And wondered why he did it.

The odd thing: he never properly knew, not really, not until later.

Once he'd started doing it, that illicit pleasure of theft and concealment, it was as though he couldn't stop. He did ponder the possibility of returning the letters at least, sneaking them into the sorting office for re-distribution. But he might be observed, or the retrospective post mark would cause suspicion; they would be linked to his round. Surely. He thought of delivering some of them again. But when it came to it, he wasn't sure if he could. Wouldn't he be compelled to take the very same?

It was the act of posting that bothered him. He didn't like pushing them into the dark vacancy of the letter box – an orifice that both appalled and enthralled him. As if he felt that by keeping the mail, particularly the hand-written envelopes, the personal gifts like the cake, he would have some kind of inkling about other lives. The lives of the people behind the doors, beyond the nets, the lit rooms like stage sets on dark mornings.

At work he appeared normal, or so he thought. It came out later, the way it does, that his colleagues had commented on his silence and heavy demeanour, his pasty face and bulbous blue eyes, his averted and hesitant gaze. Sorting offices are robust places rendering only a marginal tolerance.

One day, constipated with anxiety, the burden of the envelopes and parcels ever increasing in the front room of the flat, he decided he couldn't go in to work. He stayed in bed, pulling the covers over his head, ignoring the repeated ringing of the phone, his line manager leaving several messages. After a few days of not getting up until late afternoon, eating his way through the contents of the freezer, watching television until the small hours, he started to feel ill, stir crazy.

Summer: the ground floor flat stifling and dark, the kitchen full of the detritus of empty packets and tins, soiled cups and plates, small flies swarming from nowhere. He went out into the back yard, past the bins, the dog shit, the cat from upstairs perched on the end of the wall. Across the road a curtain twitched. A bright day, the sun in his eyes, heat beginning to build. He walked the streets for a long time, avoiding post boxes, in his head the slits of mouths in front doors watching him. Everywhere red vans passed and slowed, every other shop sold stationary or stamps, he hallucinated post offices.

Eventually he went home and opened the door of the front room with difficulty as the mass of mail had sloped towards the door jamb causing a blockage. A moment of truth – the mail was preventing him from occupying his own flat, ganging up on him. He felt out of control, terrified and sick. How had it come to this? Stealing, collecting, preserving the mail had sometimes seemed like a creative act. As if he was building connections, entering imaginatively into their world, the people in the houses with their secrets and busyness.

Some days he felt as if he cared more about their letters than they did, or would, if they ever got them. He'd seen people rip open envelopes and chuck the contents away. He would never do that. Someone had licked that envelope down; he felt the damp of their saliva still. Someone had chosen paper and spread it under her hand, chosen words to write down, like a whisper in your ear. He longed for the intimacy the hand-written envelopes suggested. The more he handled the envelopes, their papery contents, the less he wanted to push them into the dark empty spaces of the hallways.

But he felt his time was up. He'd taken too much, become too unbalanced, too outrageous in his behaviour. He thought people were watching him, sniffing him out, smelling the stink of fear. Almost two years since he'd started, he felt certain there'd been complaints from members of the public; letters that had never turned up or awaited orders. The day a curtain shifted, caught in a draught from the door. He'd not noticed but later, on the way back from getting a take-away from the Chinese place on the corner, he'd spotted a neighbour peering in, lingering by the front window. He broke into a cold sweat even though it was a warm evening.

Through the murky glass you could just make out the mound of envelopes & parcels spilled across the floor in silted disarray.

So a sense of inevitability when one morning there was a knock at the door and he saw the manager and deputy manager, uniformed and official, waiting outside. He didn't run or protest, just stood there dumbly in his stained t-shirt and pants, moving aside to let them in, watching as they entered the front room of the flat. After that things happened very quickly. The police arrived, he was arrested and charged. There were clearly doubts about his mental health but he was released on bail, put up by an Auntie who'd always had a soft spot for him. His parents removed themselves from comment or involvement.

The judge went on: irresponsibility, betrayal of trust, a depraved act not only of theft but a gross invasion of privacy; bringing the profession, the long history, of the Royal Mail into disrepute. Three years.

But how could he explain? It had started out from tenderness, for hand writing and squashy parcels, stamps stuck on wrongly, the people who moved on without leaving a forwarding address and you knew they'd never get the faithful Christmas cards and post cards from someone who wanted to keep in touch. For the lamp-lit mornings and those sweet dramas that he longed to be a part of. For the stories that each walk up the path to a door with a slit prefaced, the narrative thread he cherished. Then the increasing and appalling horror of the black rectangular maw, with its closure that snapped back like teeth. The morning he'd sat on the floor in the middle of that sea of envelopes and devoured cake, knowing his hunger, recognising for the first time his need. He couldn't tell them that either.

He was an item on the local news, not big time. After all it was a coastal town not a major city, a bit run down but still with its grand buildings. And the estates stretching back away from the centre, endlessly repeating themselves. Where he walked.

Denise McSheehy

Esme gazes at the world beyond her window.

Damned flies, leaving their crap all over the glass, she mutters. The orange-brown spots remind her of raisins in a spotted dick. She chuckles, a low throaty sound, and for a moment her face lights up. She remembers the comments her son Danny made as a child, his laughter every time someone mentioned his favourite pudding. The smile turns to a frown as she thinks of all he missed in life. He was a good soul. Too young to die. Esme sighs, shakes her head. Snap out of it woman, she thinks. Self-pity never helped anyone. Must remember to ask Bea to polish up that window.

Beatris, a pretty Hungarian student, comes for two hours a week to clean. Esme's mind fixates for a moment on what Bea had told her at her last visit and she feels ashamed. That a young girl can't go to a club without being terrorised is nothing short of a disgrace, she muses. Just because she didn't want to dance. Told to fuck off back to where she came from. Followed when she left the club. Having to ask the bouncer to call her a taxi instead of taking the night bus. Says she doesn't feel safe here any longer. Scandalous!

Esme thinks back to the first time she went to Bradford. Walking past that pub in Forster Square. A sign in the window. NO BLACKS, NO DOGS, NO IRISH. How shocked she had been. She had thought things were better, but maybe it's only a superficial improvement. Skin deep.

She sits, rheumy eyes squinting, blinking, focussing slowly. Little white clouds scud across a clear blue sky, playful, like lambs gambolling in a spring field. How she had loved to go out and walk in the spring time, watching new life emerging. A hopeful season, so much to look forward to. She remembers the early daffodils, dancing in the first spring sunshine, the warmth upon her face, restorative, wonderful. Could do with some of that now, she thinks. It's been so long…

She looks down into the street at the people scurrying around like a lot of ants. Always in such a hurry. "Slow down. Don't rush so," she says in a small voice, rusty with disuse. "Life passes by too quickly. You'll give yourselves a heart attack, end up like my Danny."

If only someone could hear me, she thinks. Invisible to the world nowadays, that's me. Didn't used to be. People used to travel for miles to see me. Lady Windermere at the Alhambra. That was a triumph. Such good reviews. Now it's me who does the watching. All the world a stage. Theatre of life and all that. Have to weave my own stories nowadays. What else is there to do? Just sitting. Gazing out on the world.

Esme hears the key in the lock. Who will it be today, she wonders?

My carers. That's what they call these people. Carers. Some care. Others don't give a monkey's. They can't get out of here quick enough. Never know who's going to turn up. Cyndy? That would be good. Whitest teeth I ever saw. Might seem so just because her skin's so dark. Black as coal. Shiny, like ebony. I like her. Always cheerful. She's huge, frightened me the first time she showed up. Waltzed in here, gave me a shock. Then she called me Mrs Hornet, not Esme like some of these whipper-snappers. I always say to them, I'm Mrs Hornet to you. But I didn't need to tell her. She's polite, efficient, gets on with the job.

"Where are you from, dear?" I asked her, to be friendly, like.

Merest flicker across her face.

"Battersea," she said. That shut me up.

"What about you Ma'am? You from round here?"

Never heard anybody call me Ma'am like that before. It's like in the movies. When I said, "Lived in this town for eighty years," she said, with a big, white, toothy smile, "Oh, you don't look old enough." Flatterer.

"Came over from Prague in '38 with the kinder transport, lived in Bethnal Green for most of my life," I tell her. "Moved into this flat ten years ago. When my husband died."

Cyndy always has me out of bed with no fuss. Felt safe with her from day one. Knows what she's doing, she does. Asks me what I want for my breakfast instead of just plonking a bowl down in front of me. When I say 'Porridge would be nice,' she makes me porridge. That first time, while she made my breakfast, she asked if I'd been back to Prague. Told her I was only eight when I came over. I never have been back.

She said, "Don't suppose you remember it then. I hope you'll tell me more of your story another day. Have to get on now, though. So sorry to rush, Ma'am. I hope I'll see you soon again."

We never had that talk. They're all in and out so fast. Have to work like the clappers.

This lunchtime it's Stan who arrives, a young man with many piercings who sings as he works, making up raps as he goes about his business.

"Morning luv," he calls as he lets himself in.

"I've told you before, I'm not your love. My name is Mrs Hornet." Esme glares at him.

He sings, or rather he chants

Ain't no one defining you,
undermining you,
by a name my dear.
Your fame is clear, my dear.
Number One, I hear
in your day.
Respect is due
to you.
So forgive me.

He bows, deep and low, and she has to laugh.

"That's better, Mrs Hornet. I'm sorry. I always forget. Most of my clients like to be called by their first names."

"Your clients? Is that what we are? Have you ever asked what they want to be called? Cos you never asked me!"

Stan looks crestfallen but only for a moment.

"No, I don't believe I have. Perhaps I should. Now let's see what you've got for your lunch."

He goes to the fridge and busies about getting grated cheese, coleslaw, cherry tomatoes, a nice soft bread roll, crème caramel. He puts it down in front of her. She tells him it's too early and he says sorry, but he has to do his rounds as they tell him to or he'll be in bother.

"I can just leave it here for you. It won't get cold, will it? You can eat it when you like," he says.

"That's why I always have salad at dinner time," she tells him.

"I know," he says. "Very sensible. Now, do you need anything else before I go?"

Esme would like to go to the bathroom, but she won't have this young boy taking her there. She has a pad on.

Think I'm incontinent, they do, but I've told them before, "If you had to wait 12 hours for someone to come and take you to the bathroom, you would be too." They tell me I don't have to wait that long, any one of them will take me if I ask, but I still have some dignity left. Better to be wet than have a boy like this wiping my privates. As long as I don't smell. What do they expect?

He leaves. Esme's mood is low now. Not his fault, she knows, but all the same. It is so frustrating being reliant on people like this. Sarah, her granddaughter, tells her she should be grateful, that some people don't get any help. One part of her agrees, but the other part screams, *Grateful? It's not as if I haven't worked hard all my life, paid my national insurance. I'm not taking up a bed anywhere. Looked after myself, I have. No drain on the NHS. I'm not fat, don't smoke, don't drink much or take drugs. I'm just old, dammit. And I can't help that. Not even allowed to choose to die. I just need a little bit of help. Is that too much to ask?*

Esme eats her salad and drinks the tea Stan made her.

He does make a good cuppa, she thinks, I'll give him that.

She switches on the TV. Another repeat. She flips through the channels and settles on Inspector Barnaby. She feels sleepy...........

"Hallo Mrs Hornet? It's Cyndy."

She jolts awake. Her neck is stiff. The TV is talking to itself.

"Hallo Cyndy dear."

"How has your day been?"

"Same as always."

"Have you had any visitors?"

"Only Stan at lunchtime."

Cyndy gets Esme her supper. Esme looks at her watch. It is only 5.30. Too early for tea let alone bed but she has no choice. Cyndy changes her nappy, helps her to put her nighty on and into bed. "Like a bloody baby," she thinks. There is such a long night ahead.

Jenny Stephen

I have a scar on the palm of my hand. But it's no ordinary scar; it's not a cut or a birthmark – it's a small grey dot that sits a couple of inches above a fuzzy brown freckle. I've had this scar since I was ten years old. But how did it get there?

Michelle was the best speller in the class. She could spell anything, and I mean *anything*.

Theatre: no problem. *Jealous*: too easy. *Ceiling*: that one would get most people, but not Michelle. Not Michelle.

I, on the other hand, was not the greatest speller. But I wanted to be. Our teacher, Miss Ashley, gave out a special prize at the end of the week to the best speller in the class. The prize was a sparkly purple pencil.

Now you might be thinking, *Why on earth would a ten-year-old boy want a sparkly purple pencil?* Well, I'll tell you.

My brother was always better than me when it came to academia. Although this would eventually change as we got older, at ten years old I was constantly bested by him. He was one of those people who possessed natural talent when it came to school work. He didn't even have to try, and yet he would still get good marks. This, as you can imagine, impressed my parents. Perhaps it gave them some sort of bragging rights amongst their friends – I don't know. My parents knew that I was different and didn't really expect all that much from me. But if I could get that pencil, it would show them.

God, it would show them.

It might not surprise you to learn that I didn't get the sparkly purple pencil that I so desperately desired. Of course, it went to Michelle – who else? Like I said, she was *always* the best speller. But I *wanted* that pencil. I *needed* that pencil.

I was fortunate enough to sit next to Michelle in class. Miss Ashley had devised an alphabetical seating plan based on our surnames. This was so that no disruptions and distractions were caused in class. If Josh was sitting next to Ollie, you knew there would be plenty of disruptions and distractions.

One day, Michelle got up from her chair and went off somewhere, leaving the pencil alone in plain sight. I just wanted to touch it, to hold it in my hand – to see what success felt like. So I picked up the pencil. I held it in my hand but was almost underwhelmed by its power – it didn't feel any different from any of the other pencils in the classroom. Maybe taking it home to show my parents wouldn't be such a big deal after all.

I was just about to put the sparkly purple pencil back on the table when I felt a sudden urge to scratch my foot. I don't know why I did this, but I put the pencil in between my sock and my shoe and started to scratch. It felt good – it felt *really* good. But as I moved the pencil back and forth, scratching away at my foot, it happened.

The pencil snapped. Not quite clean in half, but it was definitely broken. I started to panic. Michelle was on her way back to her seat, and I had the evidence right in the palm of my hand. So I did what anyone would do in that situation: I quickly placed the broken pieces of the sparkly purple pencil into my pocket before her or anyone else could see it.

Michelle came back and sat down next to me. "Where's my pencil?" she said. "I don't know," I said. "Haven't seen it."

God, I played it cool. I played it so *fucking* cool. She didn't suspect a thing. Not one *fucking* thing!

Michelle got out of her seat and rushed over to Miss Ashley, sobbing like a baby. "I can't find my pencil," she cried. "I can't find my pencil!"

We spent the whole afternoon looking for that pencil. But of course, nobody could find it. "It can't have gone far," Miss Ashley said to Michelle. "I'm sure it'll turn up eventually. See if it's at home, and if you can't find it, we can always have another look tomorrow."

The bell rang. I got out of there fast. I didn't even say goodbye to my friends – I just grabbed my bag and shot out of the door.

When I got home, I ran straight upstairs – straight to my bedroom – and shut the door. Then I took the broken pieces of pencil out of my pocket and placed them on the floor in front of me. I stared at those fragments of the sparkly purple pencil, thinking about how I was going to fix the mess that I had gotten myself into.

And then, just like that, it hit me: I'll just glue the pieces back together. She'll never know the difference. She'll *never* know the difference. I'll glue the pencil back together, take it to school, and pretend I found it on the floor – like it was just sitting there the whole entire time. What could possibly go wrong?

Of course, Michelle didn't find the pencil at home – how could she? – so as promised we all pulled together and had another look the next day at school.

After pretending to look for the pencil for a while, I was ready to do what had to be done. I waited until no-one was looking – until every single back was turned – and then I threw the pencil onto the floor. "Michelle," I said, as I bent over to pick it up. "I found it!" Then I handed the pencil over to her. "You must've dropped it," I said. There I was, playing it cool again.

She saw it immediately. She always had good attention to detail. That's what made her such an accomplished speller. It was actually rather impressive, given her age. But she didn't cry – she didn't even seem that upset about it. Instead, she took the pencil, held it tight in her fist, and with all of her force – all of her ten-year-old might – slammed the pencil down into my hand.

So that's the story of how I got the scar on the palm of my hand. I might have left out a few details, or embellished here and there, but that's the gist of it.

I don't know about you, but I like that story. In fact, it's a story that I often tell at parties or in other social situations because it always seems to get a laugh, or at the very least, a smile. But I also like that story because it helps me to remember the woman I love.

Thomas Morgan

Are we wandering down the garden path
gazing up at the Doodlebugs,
lounging in those gardens
the gardens of our paper mâché houses
all neatly arranged
on ancient flood planes?

Are we building our steeples and minarets
of china and clay
on the cliff edge
chanting
– *we are safe,*
– *we are safe?*

Are we sailing yachts
of balsa and brass
into the hurricane?
– *It's only a breeze.*
– *It's only a breeze.*
– *We'll ride the storm like our Fathers before*
and when we return, we'll build tree houses
for Ellie and Zack
deep in the forest,
where they can build fires
from desert-dry sticks
and toast marshmallows in safety.

Are we riding into the eye of the storm,
when we could escape through the eye of the needle,
if only we were prepared to pay the price,
or would we rather sacrifice

our glaciers,
polar bears,
island nations,
Rotterdam,
Amsterdam,
New York,
London,
our Forests,

forsake proven science for gung-ho foolery?

Are we wandering down the garden path
in paper hats,
singing songs,
throwing confetti
and dancing beneath the Doodlebugs?

Note: In 1944, during WWII, flying bombs – known as Doodlebugs – were launched at London; my Granddad was deaf and hadn't heard about these new weapons, so when one flew overhead, he wandered down the garden path gazing up in fascination.

Richard Cave

Mrs Tipper chooses me to start the counting. I stand at my desk in my best dress and the other children turn to watch.

"One, two, three, thour –"

"Four," shouts Mrs Tipper, "F F Four." She has white hairs sprouting from her chin and smells like dusty rose petals in a bowl on a windowsill.

The desk is that dark wood colour of old things, scratched deep and inky blue from the old children, and the top of the desk has an inkwell made from brown plastic like the wireless. After lunch I used to lie on the sofa with my mummy for *Listen with Mother* and the funny dry smell of the wireless. But now I'm a big girl at school for dinners.

"One, two, free, four –"

"Three! Th Th Three."

My dress is red and yellow roses on a pale green background. My mummy's having a baby and I'm staying with Lindy and Lindy's mummy doesn't know I'm not allowed to wear this dress to school. I look pretty in it. The shape of one of the roses, if I stare hard, is like a baby's face. Maybe I'll see our baby tonight.

"One, two, three, four, thive –"

"Sit down, your tongue's all a twist. Who can show her?"

I know! I know! I want to shout but I can't in case I cry. Daddy came to Lindy's house last night with lines on his face like extra eyebrows. He said we should be patient and pray for the baby – I must be good and make him proud of me. I want him proud and of course I can count. It's just, in front of everyone like that.

Our first day back after Christmas and Mrs Tipper gathers us round the blackboard for sums. The sun comes through the window and lands in a pool on the shiny dark floor and you can see the chalk dust dancing, dry in your throat. I stand next to Jeanie Draper. She's smaller than me with thin brown hair in a ponytail and a green ribbon. A long thread from the ribbon wiggles down her back. Jeanie Draper started school the same time as me, but she still can't do counting. Jeanie Draper smells of cabbage.

Mrs Tipper raps her ruler on the blackboard, and I try to pay attention.

"If I have two sweets in one hand..." She writes a big *2* on the board with a new piece of chalk. It squeaks as it does the curly bit. "...and four sweets in the other hand..." she writes a *4* a bit away from the *2* "...how many sweets do I have altogether?" She draws a plus sign between the *2* and the *4*.

I count on my fingers behind my back. One, two – three, four, five, six. Like when I found the sixpence in Daddy's pocket after the baby didn't come. I bought six penny chews and made myself feel sick and the sweetshop lady told Mummy.

Mrs Tipper points the ruler at Jeanie. Jeanie hangs her head and a bit of hair has come out of her ponytail over her face.

"Jeanie Draper? How many sweets?" Mrs Tipper's eyes are big and bulgy under her glasses and her bushy eyebrows twitch.

"I don't know." Jeanie's voice is like a grey mouse. Mrs Tipper grabs Jeanie's wrists. She takes the ruler and taps the hands as she says the sum again.

"Two sweets in *this* hand – four sweets in *this* hand. One. Two. How many?"

I want to whisper but I daren't. Jeanie's face is the colour of the pastry I roll out with the set Mummy gave me for Christmas.

"Five," she squeaks, and I know she's guessing. Mrs Tipper hits the hands harder as she counts out the sweets.

"One. Two. – Three. Four. Five. Six."

The ruler makes a whizzy noise each time before the whack and Jeanie does little hurting jumps.

I haven't been a good girl to make my daddy proud, but I will always be sure to get my sums right.

I stand in the corner, feet together, shoulders straight, hands in front like I'm praying. Eyes shut. I can hear the children outside, the slap of the skipping rope – *vote vote vote for dear old Christine*. Inside the clock ticktocks so slowly and Mrs Tipper and the vicar are talking but I can't hear what they're saying. The back of my ankle itches and I long to scratch it with my other foot. And I long long to open my eyes, just a tiny peep, but I don't dare because they are watching, and I am a naughty bad dis-spectful girl.

Winston Churchill has died, and he was a great man because he was very old and fat and he won the war and if it wasn't for Winston Churchill Hitler would be king and we would all be slaves. When Mummy was a girl she was scared of Hitler under her bed, and if it wasn't for Winston Churchill Hitler would be under my bed now. Today the vicar came to do a special assembly and made us stand, eyes closed, hands together, silent for two minutes. I didn't mind the silence which sounds like tick-tock and different sorts of breathing, but I couldn't help looking at the rows of shoes in front of me. Some brown, some black, some worn out red. One pair of shiny party shoes. I wonder if she's allowed or if her mummy's having a baby? She'd better pray hard or there'll be no baby. She had white socks pulled up neat, but the other socks were grey and falling down and some falling down more than others and if I screwed my eyes, I could muddle up the feet and not be sure which two went together. The church bell sounded from across the school yard, and I counted up to eleven and then the vicar called out my name and it bounced around in all that silence and it took me to fifteen to realise he meant me and what a disgrace, on this day, that one little girl wouldn't close her eyes for the memory of a Great National Hero.

This is my punishment. To stand here all through playtime, hands together, eyes closed, and think about Winston Churchill. I saw him on Lindy's television, and he made me think of a baby with his big fat face. Lindy's mummy said all babies look like Churchill but then she snapped her lips shut and turned away from me. Maybe our baby looked like Churchill, but it won't be a Great National Hero or anything.

Perhaps it was a Blessing, the poor little soul, I heard sweetshop lady say. When Daddy put seed in Mummy's tummy to make a baby – was it a Blessing? Mummy lies alone on the sofa now with the curtains drawn and no wireless on. I have to be a Grown-Up Girl to make Mummy proud, but she won't be proud of me today wanting to itch my ankle so badly and my skin all prickly and hot and dirty.

Where do the babies go when you don't pray hard enough for them? I want to ask, but I'm scared of the answer. Prayers are not the same as wishes, you can wish for anything when you blow out birthday candles, like lemonade rivers and sweets on the trees, or being a princess or a fairy. Prayers are for making sad things better, but you have to be good for them to work, and even then, we can't make Winston Churchill alive again, can we?

There are dinner smells coming from the kitchen and I guess it will be stew and dumplings. My tummy feels hollow even though I'm not hungry and I wish I felt sorry and sad about Churchill and I wish I could be always always good and pray the babies back.

Penny Frances

It could almost have been the school motto: *Shorts to toughen the constitution, Latin to toughen the mind.*
We used to go to school in shorts all year round. Grey corduroy shorts, come rain or shine, summer, winter, even when it was snowing. Even in a hail storm. Well actually I think hail storms were where they drew the line. But you get the picture. I hated wearing them at first – but they grew on you. And grew on you. Like fungus I suppose. Until in the end you didn't give a damn anymore.
The school was called Rhodes – a prep school tucked away in the woods near a village in Hampshire. It was me and my younger brother – it was the first English school we had ever been to and we were both terrified. My parents had sold the house in Ireland in the summer of 1979 and moved to England, where we spent three months living in a caravan in Pirbright while they hunted for a house. The camping experience started out as an adventure but after a month of it we'd had enough. We just wanted to get back to civilization.
But the weeks rolled on and still there was no sign of the house. My father said he'd already bought it, but it took a long time to sort the deeds out. I didn't know what deeds were, nor did I care. I got to the point where I wanted to roll the caravan off the edge of a cliff and watch it smash into pieces on the rocks below.
But finally the day came. Finally the house was ready, a fancy four bedroom Victorian house with a double garage and a huge garden as it turned out, in a small village called Barkham. We packed up the caravan and moved in. A few weeks later it was time to go to school.
We were day pupils at first. After a year and a half we boarded. I was afraid of the school at first. I had figured that English schools were somehow better than Irish ones. Superior in some way, that's what I thought. But thinking back on it, nothing was further from the truth. The teaching wasn't better, it was just done differently. And most of the school teachers were complete eccentrics.
Like Mr Melville, our maths teacher and the world's first rechargeable member of staff. He had a strange, clanky, mechanical walk and used to struggle getting upstairs. Rumour had it that he was battery-powered, half robot, a cyborg of some kind. He was a highly intelligent man and was involved in maths research projects, but sometimes it seemed like he'd had a malfunction and he would stare out at the class blankly. We used to joke that he just needed rebooting, but he would explain it was because he was a little absentminded and was just thinking a complex problem through.
With Mr Melville, the standard class dare was to try to escape from the classroom when he wasn't looking and see if he actually noticed. One day in Autumn it was baking hot in the classroom, so Mr Melville told us to

open all the windows. Then, while he was scrawling the next problem on the black board, we edged ourselves closer and closer to the windows and then a boy called Jennings climbed out of one of the windows and was gone. Then another boy, and another boy, and another. Until finally Mr Melville swung round and surveyed the class. As usual, he seemed detached, lost in a mathematical world of his own. He didn't appear to notice that half of the class had gone.

He returned to his work on the blackboard, at which point Jennings appeared at the classroom door, crept back in and sat down at his desk. Then one by one, while Mr Melville's back was still turned, the rest of the boys crept back in and did likewise. Somehow they got away with it. Mr Melville didn't bat an eyelid.

Then there was Mr Jarvis, our history teacher. A huge man with a mane of jet black hair who looked like Bill Sykes, he smoked a pipe and always wore the same gray tweed jacket that reeked of tobacco. He had a furious temper and was a truly terrible teacher. Each lesson he would greet us briefly, then tell us to go to our desks and sit down. Then he would turn his back on the class and write out whole pages of history notes on the board, instructing us to copy it down word for word and commit the whole thing to memory. That was it. No class discussion, no interaction, nothing at all.

But the worst thing about him was his temper.

As with all the teachers, he helped out with games. One summer we all went up to the sports field a few miles north of the school to play hockey. The game was all going swimmingly until a boy called Parker starting goofing around with the hockey ball, trying to score own goals. Mr Jarvis yelled across the pitch at him, ordering him to stop acting the fool, but Parker just ignored him and carried on hitting the ball into the goal.

Mr Jarvis yelled across at him again and gave him a final warning. Parker deliberately smacked the ball into the goal again, thrilled that he was really annoying the hell out of Mr Jarvis now.

At which point Mr Jarvis snapped.

He grabbed a hockey stick from one of the other boys, swung it round and round and finally flung it headlong across the pitch at Parker. It soared across the pitch like a boomerang and struck Parker square on the shins. He crashed to the ground in agony, screaming out, clutching his legs. We all just froze and stood there in shock. Mr Jarvis marched over to him, stood over him and told him to get up.

But Parker couldn't do it. He tried to get up, stood up awkwardly but then just crashed to the floor in pain. Mr Jarvis told him to stop faking it, but then Mr Melville marched up to him and tapped him on the shoulder. Mr Jarvis swung round and they had a blazing row while Parker lay there on the ground. Finally Mr Jarvis looked down again at the boy, his face still simmering with anger but now racked in shame. Then he lifted him up and carried him to his car. He asked Mr Melville to take charge of the hockey match and drove Parker back to school.

But of all of the teachers, the most bizarre teacher we had was Mr Grimstone – a tall, lank-haired eccentric academic with a gravelly voice who reminded me of Ted Hughes. He was our Latin teacher and was obviously fanatical about the subject. He used to talk for hours about how Latin was the grandfather of all languages and was by far the most important subject we would ever study. It was, he said, the best subject for training young minds.

He would ramble on about Julius Caesar, the emperor Augustus and other heroes from long ago and then he would say that he would have preferred to have lived in those times. We wished he had as well, to be honest. He was like a lumbering old dinosaur. We often joked that if only we could bungle him into a time machine and send him back to Roman times, he'd get eaten by a pack of lions and we'd never have to see the old fool again. But in the end we just put up with him as best we could.

During one class in the spring of 1979, Mr Grimstone was boring us senseless with another rendition of "Veni, Vidi, Vici" until he agreed that we'd got that now.

So he moved on to talk about what had happened in the aftermath of Caesar's death. He said there was a phrase in Latin which the emperor Augustus had used a lot. It was called "in praecepto", he said, and he wanted to give the class an example of its usage. He got all animated at this point and broke out into one of his creepy smiles as he looked out across the class.

"So – can anyone tell me what 'in praecepto' means?"

We all looked at him blankly, wondering what on earth he was talking about.

"Oh come on, chaps. You're a clever bunch aren't you? Surely you can have a guess?"

Still silence. He looked across at Hathaway, who usually sat near the front of the class and was one of the boys who got more involved.

"Hathaway? Any ideas?"

"Well, no, not really sir. A bit lost, to be honest."

"Right. In praecepto. This is the point in history just after Julius Caesar has been killed. He was emperor of the Roman Empire, so they had to appoint a successor! Just have a guess!"

"I have no idea, sir. Nothing comes to mind."

Mr Grimstone started getting impatient. He started rolling his hands together.

"Well, Caesar had no children. So, he had adopted Augustus Octavius to be his successor, IN PRAECEPTO the Roman Empire. Does that help?"

Hathaway looked even more baffled now. He scratched his head.

"No sir."

"Well, it means 'To be ...' "

Hathaway frowned at him. "Sorry sir?"

Mr Grimstone tried again, his voice now a low growl.

"In praecepto. It means to be ... to be ..."

"To be what?"

"To be .... to be .... to be in ...."

Hathaway's expression brightened a little.

"To be in battle?"

Mr Grimstone slammed his fist on his desk, sending clouds of chalk dust swirling up into the air.

"No! No! To be in ... to be in c ..... to be in c ...."

A boy called Sherwood piped up and called out from the back of the class.

"To be in Coventry?"

At this point Mr Grimstone exploded.

"No! No! No you imbecile! Why would it mean Coventry?! This is ancient Rome!!"

He crossed to the windows and opened one of them, gasping for air. He stayed there for a few moments, trying to get a grip on himself. Then finally he turned his attention back to Hathaway.

"Ok. I give up. It means 'To be in command of'. That's what 'in praecepto' means!"

His face was shaking as he explained this. His face and neck had turned bright red and the veins on his neck had turned purple. It struck me that he looked like a human volcano, like he might spontaneously combust at any moment. I'd never seen anyone in such a state.

"Honestly, sometimes I wonder whether I can teach you lot anything at all!"

And with that, he got up from his desk, went to the door and flung it open. He stormed out of the class and didn't come back. And after that, no-one saw him ever again.

But the irony was that we never forgot what "in praecepto" meant. If there is one thing that I remember from all my Latin classes, then Julius Caesar, the emperor Augustus and "to be in command of" is it.

Paul Saville

Benjamin Britten

LABURNUM

Jaundice flower
its lips slightly parted

as if I would
as if I would

a child brushes
past and grabs

a hand of
toxic pods

pops seeds like peas –

just hours later comes
the crushing sleep

the fever
vomiting
the coma

the slow stagger into night
and the reach

of the surgeon's
stomach pump.

        The teacher stood
before the school

described the shame
stupidity

of the unnamed child
and though we tried

our best to find out
which one of us it was

we never did.

C. M. Buckland

FIRST VIRGINS   Not behind the bike sheds
                 but in the school loos where,
                 when wet behind the ears,
                 we fagged for demigods
                 of the Sixth or Prefects,
                 black as Corvids. We warmed
                 the toilet seats or hid
                 their secret hoard of fags
                 from sleek-gowned, eagle-eyed,
                 hawk-nosed flocks of teachers.

                 Now we three – Gals, Barney,
                 Myself – crouch in shared prayer
                 round this red phallic tip:
                 a King Size No. 6,
                 with all the bravado,
                 the rude insouciance,
                 of Virginia virgins,
                 thumbs in pockets, sullen,
                 with the studied swagger
                 of Jagger or Lennon.

                 After the last heeled butt
                 we pray our V'd fingers
                 are capstan-tanned, new-badged
                 with nicotine, not this
                 dizzy tingling rush, this
                 knotted sick-to-the-pit.
                 At the first warning caw
                 we dissipate like mist,
                 emerge mint-breathed, sucking
                 on an infinite O.

                 Marek Urbanowicz

I was eighteen. Old enough to vote. Though I never had. Old enough to marry. Though I'd never been on a real date. Old enough to die for my country (people still talked like that back then). *But why the fuck would you?* as Pete liked to say. And I'd only been abroad once, to Paris on a school trip. We'd marveled at the French girls, their flawless skin and flawless French. Eighteen, just. A virgin, of course. About to become a student when being a student meant you were a bit special. I'd bought a donkey jacket from Millet's with my first wage packet. We were a new wave. I was on the edge of the rest of my life.

I'd got a summer job in the supermarket that had just opened up on the site of the demolished shoe factory. It'd come out like a blackened tooth. If you couldn't work, at least you could shop. It was the future. They only had one music tape when the shop opened – Stevie Wonder's *Greatest Hits* – and it drove us crazy all summer. It was nineteen seventy-six and there were a gang of us, getting ready to leave home for the first time like swallows on the wire, febrile with the sense of change. Mainly, there was me and Pete.

We spent our days stocking shelves or wheeling trolleys in the warehouse. Maybe a stint on the bacon counter with its smell of cold grease, the women mocking our long hair. *Bloody hell, lad, you favour a mop head!* Then a couple of pints before going home as the evening light streamed through the windows of the Sun Mill Inn. The beer flowed through half-measure pumps at the bar like liquefied gold. The lads from the engineering works jumped up on the tables in stained overalls, swung their hips and pumped their fists to the beat of Gary Glitter. *Come on! Come on!*

Long days started at seven a.m., clocking-on in the smell of detergent that still reminds me of those days. That moment slotting the card into the machine, a whole day of work ahead. Time mortgaged. Stacking shelves for two hours before the shop opened, the aisles empty of shoppers. Filling the gaps until everything was in place again. It was timeless. A cornucopia of never-ending plenty in a town that had been dying for as long as I'd lived there. And that sound track: *Shoo- be-doo-be-doo-da-day.*

About a week into the job I was dragging another pack of tinned beans from the forklift, slicing it open with a Stanley knife.

"You'll have to move a bit quicker than that to keep Jackson off your back!"

Then that quiet chuckle.

"Move them up two at a time."

Linda crouched down beside me, our shoulders touching. She wore the blue suit of a supervisor. I caught the scent of perfume, felt her hair brush my face. It was blonde and she wore it in a bob.

"Like this, see?"

She swung two cans with one hand. Out from the pack and onto the shelf, then did it again, then again. I gave it a try and dropped a can, denting the rim. She tutted theatrically and pushed it to the back of the shelf.

"You won't be studying retail sales, then?"

"History and Politics."

Linda pretended to be impressed but she was laughing at me.

She came just a little higher than my shoulder. Dimpled. A little cleft in her chin. She had even teeth, as if she'd worn a brace when she was a kid. She didn't use makeup. Her eyes were green, and I was blushing. Pete was stacking breakfast cereals further down the aisle and smirking across at us. Then Linda was turning away to spare me, her calves brisk above flat-heeled shoes that might have seemed staid on anyone else. But not on Linda. On Linda they looked just right. They looked tasteful.

She must have been twenty-eight, though she seemed younger. She had a way of getting the best out of everyone without hassling you. Unlike Jackson, who was a twat of the first order, as Pete liked to say, declaiming from one of the stacks in the warehouse, fingering his new beard, his dark hair falling over his shoulder as Irish Lil the tattooed cleaner cursed him.

"You useless feckin' gobshite!"

Pete put his fingers in his mouth and wolf-whistled back at her, until she delivered the ultimate indictment.

"Cunt!"

Catharsis achieved, Pete was delighted. No one messed with Lillian, but Pete seemed to get away with it. We'd been friends since primary school when we'd sat next to each other. He was a Twomey and I was a Tattersall. Then surviving grammar school where we both kept our heads down, where we were processed rather than educated. The headmaster bullied the teachers, the teachers bullied us, we bullied each other. And we bullied the teachers when we could. The nice ones didn't stand a chance. Now the supermarket, where days passed in the boredom of work. Clocking on at seven a.m., clocking off at five; getting a taste of the world of work just to remind us what we were escaping.

The town had been on its arse ever since I'd known it, the rotting cradle of industry. The old mills were empty, their chimneys coming down, collapsing into dust and debris, making headlines in the local paper. There was a future in demolition, at least. The shoe factory was gone. The pottery where Pete's mum worked went bankrupt and the stock was sold off. The linen mill was home to a new gym and a couple of mail order companies. Corner shops closed as the factories closed. Lines of workers who'd queued in overalls for bacon butties or corned beef sandwiches had vanished. It was a town of ghosts. *The Undead*, Pete called them.

Then the supermarkets and shopping centres came to strip off the last meat from the bone. Retail outlets. The town, once famous for manufacturing became famous for unemployment and racial violence. A minor riot had started in a pub called The Goodfellows when some Asian guy got glassed by a crypto-fascist. That said it all. *Crypto what?* Linda said laughing at us in the canteen. *They're just arseholes, aren't they?* So, when I say *us*, I really mean me and Pete, who'd grown a Ché Guevara beard and was heading for Reading University to study philosophy. Another reason Lillian thought he was a cunt.

I lived with my mum and dad and a cat called Marmalade in a semi-detached house on a Council estate built in the fifties. It had replaced an infamous slum, pulled down after the war when the town got a Labour Council. I'd never lived anywhere else. My parents were both locals. They'd met at a dinner dance in the days before rock and roll. It was hard to imagine. My parents dancing to a swing band or a string quartet.

We had a beige Austin Maxi and an asbestos garage that, in point of fact, was perfectly safe. A garden with a square lawn and privet hedge and rockery and a lattice fence to separate us from the neighbours. They cooked some kind of foreign food in the evenings when we left the windows open to cool the house and blackbirds sang from garden to garden. *Curry.* Said with a sniff and a toss of the head as my mum set about liver and bacon, slamming the HP sauce on the table for my dad to slather over everything. She always seemed cross with him. A state of perpetuity. Just like the way we'd always lived there.

My mum worked as a school secretary and my dad was a clerical officer at the magistrate's court, though he'd been a police cadet for a time before I came along. You couldn't imagine that, either. My dad in a uniform and helmet. Radio protocols. *Roger, over and out.* The long arm of the law. He had serious hair loss and used to rub Bay Rum into his scalp. It smelled of cloves and desperation. They must have loved each other once, but their lips squeezed together like traps whenever anything like that came up on TV.

Mostly, I didn't want to imagine any of that stuff, listening to Hendrix and Led Zeppelin and T Rex on Radio Caroline in bed, thinking about girls. Thinking about Linda, actually, who was much more than a girl. I wanted it to pass: childhood, adolescence. The teenage years of yawning boredom and repetition and tellings-off from parents and teachers and rubber-necking neighbours if you so much as farted in the garden when they were lying in their deckchairs, shutting out the smell of chicken tikka masala from *you know where.* They were hoping they'd be proved right about things. The miners. The anti-apartheid mob. Anyone who was bolshie. Anyone with bell bottoms or hair touching their collar. We wanted to prove them wrong. Me and Pete, who had a pair of velvet loons and a paisley waistcoat.

That summer my parents went on holiday to a B&B on the Pembrokeshire coast and left me alone for two weeks. It had never happened before and you could tell my dad didn't like it one little bit. But then I had a job and was earning money for the first time in my life and that meant something. To them and to me. It stood for something. I could cook simple dishes – omelettes and casseroles with a tin of steak – so I wouldn't starve. The nice neighbours, Geoff and Edith, had a key. In case I left the gas on or wanked myself to death, I suppose. My mum looked upset when they were leaving, leaning from the window of the car to remind me about locking the back door at night. As if the Sikh family who lived opposite would swarm through the garden under cover of darkness with the knives they kept hidden in their turbans. I could be murdered by bus conductors before my life had really started. You had to hand it to her.

The other thing about Linda was crosswords. Pete and I laboured through the Daily Mirror in our tea-breaks. Whenever she was around she was a dab hand at supplying us with the most perplexing words. She got *mainmast, perturbation* and *watercress* in one session, leaving us with one clue to go. *Sixth form English,* she said, smoothing down her skirt and straightening her name tag, winking at Pete as she left. *Sort that last one out yourselves.* Six across, five letters: *Mediterranean jellyfish.*

Pete wasn't the slightest bit interested in girls. But you didn't talk about being gay back then. Not in our town. Not if you had any sense. Not if you had a head to kick in. That was a cross he had to carry for a bit longer. One that he'd eventually lay down when we were hitching in Spain after graduation. Before they had gap years, which we'd never heard of, and everyone did it. I told him about Linda on that trip, too. Sitting up in the tent with our gas light, drinking red wine from a NATO water bottle I'd bought at the Army and Navy shop, eating squashed baguette, our shadows cast against the nylon as if we were giants.

In both cases it was probably the wine that loosened up the past. We had our degrees. I'd got a Two-One. Pete had got a First and was about do an MA. My Mum wanted to know why I wasn't doing an MA, when you could get a maintenance grant. Remember those? I didn't know what I wanted to do, to be honest. Pete and I hadn't seen each other that much in three years and were finding out just what had changed about us. If anything ever really changes. *Comes to the surface* might be a better expression. Things rise up that are sometimes better forgotten. But not always. It wasn't all about the future. We were reminiscing about that summer before we finally left home, the way young people do. Squatting on our sleeping bags, slugging back the wine. Even then, just into my twenties, I was full of longing for the past.

I'd been back to the supermarket, getting ready to seem surprised, wandering the aisles, dangling a basket, pretending to shop. But Linda was long gone. She was far too smart to stand still in one place. There was a West Indian family in her little house, the kids laughing at me curiously when I knocked on the door to ask for her. The mother bustling through to say she was gone. *Sorry,* she said, smiling sorrowfully, *we're sorry fer real.* As if someone had died. When that had been my dad in my third year, canary-yellow with pancreatic cancer. My mum completely lost without him.

Back in seventy-six, it was a hot summer. A blistering summer in a stifling little town where the slate roofs seemed to soak up the heat and you lay awake at night sticking to the sheets and pillows. Sometimes, in the late afternoons after work, I went swimming in the local baths. They'd been built before most houses had bathrooms. Slipper baths. Turkish baths. It was all a bit mysterious, but it was the pool I was interested in with its chilly waters and tang of chlorine and yelling kids, their mothers cruising. I'd take my towel and swimming shorts into work. Pete would rather have jumped off a high building than go swimming. But there I was, not wanting to go home, counting the hours to when I could clock off.

I was a pretty hopeless swimmer, but it passed the time, and it was cool. And there were girls. It was always pretty crowded there and you had to make way carefully, crawling down the length of the baths, the blue tiles wavering and glimmering, the hubbub closing over you. It didn't take much to put me off my stroke so I'd be spitting chlorine. One day, something or someone shot into the water beside me and overtook me with rapid, efficient strokes. When I got to the other end, Linda was grinning at me, her hair plastered to her head. She ducked down below the surface, emerged again like something reborn, then set off with the breaststroke. Lazily powerful. Her shoulders creamy in the filtered light. Later I noticed her on the diving board in her black one-piece costume, her body neat and compact, knifing into the water.

I wondered if she'd come here as a kid, like I did with my mum. Shivering at the cold, drinking hot Bovril in the café. I decided to get out of the way before she saw how useless I was. But she didn't hang about either.

"Well, well!"

She was strolling towards me as I waited for my bus, her swimming kit dangling in an orange carrier bag. Jeans. A man's collarless shirt.

"Do you?"

"What?"

"Come here often?"

Her eyes wide with mock surprise.

"Not really, I'm a crap swimmer."

"You are, I couldn't help noticing."

She was teasing me again. I must have blushed because she touched my arm.

"I could teach you."

There was my bus approaching.

"I don't think *anyone* could teach me ..."

"No maybe not ..."

A group of school kids pushed past us with their satchels. I pulled myself up onto the platform, wondering if she'd follow. But she stayed put, pushing the bracelet of her watch up her arm. She looked nervous, for the first time.

"I'll see you, then."

"See you later ..."

I wish I'd thought of something smart to say. *Alligator?* My Mum used to say that. It was what you said to kids. I noticed Linda didn't wear a wedding ring. She didn't seem afraid of anything, but she grew smaller as the bus pulled away.

My parents left on Saturday, my day off. Mum was fussing about everything as my dad packed the car. He was fanatical about anything rattling in the back. He was trying to pretend that leaving me on my own for two weeks was nothing special. I had money to pay the milkman, I had to pick up the papers, which my Dad usually did on his way to work. I'd need to remember to get some shopping and not live on takeaways or the chip shop. I waved them off. That first night alone was eerie. Pete came across and we turned up the radiogram. He was getting into King Crimson and Free and Curved Air. It was strange being in charge. It felt like the end of something and the start of something. But I had absolutely no idea what. I can't remember what we talked about, either. It was just another moment in our long conversation about leaving.

I do remember that on Sunday I was working again. Leaving our empty house, which was a weird feeling at first. In those days, supermarkets closed on Sundays and it was a day of shelf stocking, stocktaking, getting ready for the Monday rush. Linda was on duty and she came to work dressed in casual clothes. A pair of old jeans and sneakers and a tennis shirt that looked as if it'd seen action on the court.

She told me once she'd been to the Girls Grammar School, just after slotting some crossword clue into place with mock triumph. Pete and I had been to the boys' one, before they merged with the girls as a co-ed comprehensive. If you were good at metalwork they marched you down to engineering drawing. I scraped through with French 'O' level and a clutch of other subjects, which sent me down the other route: English, Geography and History.

The shop was always quiet on Sundays, like trespassing in an empty church. And, thank God, Stevie Wonder was turned off. It was the day most stuff went missing, Jackson had once said, significantly, eyeing us up as we stretched out our tea break.

"Like we'd nick anything from this shithole."

Pete slung his tea bag into the sink and let water run into his cup.

"Instant coffee, toilet paper, nappy sterilizer, tampons, pre-cooked pastry cases, Weetabix, family pack ... "

Pete flicked his cup upside down.

"...oh yes, the list is endless, Jackson."

But Jackson had already gone and Linda was there with her quizzical smile, hands on hips, as if she didn't quite get us.

As it happened, Pete was off work that Sunday, so the day dragged more than usual. Linda and I did the crossword together in an empty canteen, our heads almost touching over the table. The scent of her hair wafted close, her eyelashes flickering in concentration. Her closeness, the warmth of her skin, a faint perfume I could never quite place. Her neat hands on the biro, filling out the clues or scribbling a word in the margins. The frank green eyes that seemed to be narrowed at me the whole time, as if she was holding back laughter.

In the afternoon I did a stint in the warehouse arranging pallets. Heavy work. I was resting on the handle of the truck when I felt someone come up behind me and slide something into the back pocket of my jeans. By the time I turned around, they'd slipped away down one of the aisles. I didn't have time to think about it because Jackson was on the prowl, putting us under pressure just for the sake of it.

"Come on Michael, we don't pay you to pat your arse."

I did the wide-eyed look.

"Get on with it!"

He had a stupid moustache, a whippet's stomach and Terylene flares. I pressed the lever to lower the forks and the pallet sank to the floor as he watched me. By the time I'd shifted the rest of the delivery I'd forgotten about whatever it was in my pocket. I remembered Linda blanking me as we clocked off at four-pm, but I thought nothing of it. She just looked a bit preoccupied.

I was waiting for my bus, standing in the sunshine we'd missed, when I felt in my pocket for change. I found a slip of paper. It had *Linda* written on one side and her address and something else written on the other. *Twenty-seven, Boar Hill St. Seven o'clock.* My chest went tight. Linda's hand-writing slanted to the right. We'd been taught it should slant the other way. When I looked up, the bus was there, panting diesel into the heat, the conductor looking at me from the platform as if I was an idiot.

I could see a faint reflection of myself in the window as we bumped towards home. I kept telling myself that I was eighteen. Eighteen. I remember telling my younger cousin when he was nine that I'd been nine once. He'd looked at me as if I was nuts. *Everyone used to be nine,* he said, as if it was blindingly obvious. Now everyone used to be seventeen.

Boar Hill Street was down by the stinking grey river in the old town. Cobbled streets radiated down from the parish church that stood on a little hill, its stone darkened by soot and rain. I knew where it was because my mum's mother had lived nearby. She ran a little sweet shop from her front room and we'd visited when I was a kid, my mum leaving me with her sometimes to go shopping or visit the doctor with some ailment they spoke about in whispers. Seven o'clock. That left just over two hours. My gran had found me stealing sweets once and slapped my legs.

I got home and ran the bath. My mum had ironed a few shirts for me and I chose an old blue one, made out of crisp cotton poplin. My favourite jeans were clean and I remember standing at the sink scrubbing my teeth, watching the cat stalking something in the garden. Mum had bought me a deodorant stick after one of our little talks and I lashed it on. Old Spice, with a picture of a sailing ship on the label. I sat in in a deckchair after that, watching the sun dip behind the neighbour's greenhouse, killing time.

Linda. She was half my age again. Beyond that fact, nothing was obvious. She'd chosen her moment. I must have let drop that my parents were away. Accidentally-on-purpose. Tomorrow was my day off and I was pretty sure it would be hers. It was a ten-minute walk to Boar Hill Street when I finally left the house, putting down some milk for the cat which was rubbing against my legs. There were jet trails across the sky, converging somewhere beyond the town. Somewhere that wasn't England. I waited until the sun fell behind the laburnum tree. It trailed remnants of yellow blossom like streamers left over from a party. Every part of it was poisonous, my dad had told me. Locking the house felt like a betrayal. I didn't know why.

Linda's house had net curtains in the sashes and a dark maroon door. There was an old watering can planted with flowers outside. The house was one of the two-up two-down terraces with a kitchen and bathroom added on where the back yard and the old long-drop toilet had been. There was a brass knocker, no bell. I could hear footsteps thudding softly as she came down the stairs that spilled into the little hallway. She smiled at me and pulled the door wider. She'd changed into a summer frock, deep crimson with yellow flowers and blue parakeets. She was barefoot.

"Hi! Come in."

She sounded surprised, as if none of this had been arranged. I followed her, noticing the freckles on her shoulders, a trace of talcum powder. The front room had a plain three-piece suite and a coffee table laid out with two glasses and a bottle of wine that I recognized from the supermarket.

"This is nice."

"We do our best!"

She smiled again, flicking a wing of hair back from her face. Her arms were bare and sun tanned and I could see a paler stripe where her wristwatch had been. Showers were rare in those days, so I guessed she'd just got out of the bath.

There was a bowl of olives on the table, something I'd never tasted, but recognized from stocking the fridges. The open fire had been replaced with a gas fire and in one alcove was a Philips Dansette record player. There was a line of swimming trophies on the mantelpiece and a cup with crossed tennis racquets. The other alcove was lined with books and records. The last rays of the sun made a faint haze as they fell though the net curtains that shielded us from the street. I watched Linda go to the record player and drop the needle onto an LP. The room thrummed to the chords of flamenco guitar. Then she was pouring the wine and I was perching on the edge of the settee. I couldn't really describe how I was feeling. We never had wine at home. I'd only ever tasted it at family weddings or christenings. As she stooped, I could see a cascade of freckles above her breasts.

You can guess the rest. How there was an awkward silence as we sat with dry mouths, not saying much. How the wine mixed with the slight bitterness of the olives. How we shifted closer on the settee until our bodies were touching and how our breath quickened as the music stopped and the stylus clicked and I was kissing her, tasting her, fumbling with the buttons on her frock. How the bed was neatly made with clean cotton sheets and how she guided me that first time when I came too soon, then waited patiently, then guided me again until we were moving together and her body was the only thing I'd ever wanted, kissing her breasts and lips, her eyes closing, my hand under her waist as we made love with the last light of the sun rosy against the bleak parish church that filled the top quarter of the window.

Then how we dozed, waking hot and sticky, until she kicked off the sheets and we cooled together, my face nuzzling her clean-smelling hair, our fingers and legs intertwined. Then it was chilly, and she pulled the sheets back and we lay together as darkness sifted into the room and the streetlights burned yellow like the cats' eyes the length of the street. There should have been a faint sickle of moon with that old cynical smile of approval as the world turned under it. But if there was, I never saw it. Not until I was walking home in the early hours, before the town was fully awake.

In the morning the room was dark and the light lemon-coloured on the sycamores under the church. There were sparrows squabbling in the gutters and when I woke she was still sleeping, her lips pressing together and relaxing as if she wanted to say something. Then she woke and pulled on some knickers and went to the loo. Then I did, slipping into my jeans, then slipping them off again to get back into bed. We held each other, her breasts soft against my chest. I kissed them and put my hand on her belly, but she pushed it away.

"Not now, we'll be sore!"

I put my lips to her throat and felt the blood beating there. She laughed, pushing at my head.

"You're sweet ..."

She kissed the tip of my nose.

"But trust me."

And I did. I was about to speak, but she put her finger against my lips and said.

"Not now. Tonight. There's always tonight, sweetheart."

Sweetheart. She said it plainly and simply with a Lancashire burr that made her sound so sensible. *Sweetheart.* Like a fact. Like something incontrovertible, obvious, something in plain sight.

But she was right. There was Monday night and every night for the next two weeks, as long as my parents were away. I left the house lights on at home for the neighbours' sake. Staying over at Linda's, walking home light-headed through empty streets as the milk floats were at work, filling up empty doorsteps across the town, the bottles clinking softly. Most days the cat was already waiting for me and I'd feed him in the kitchen, rinsing the tin clean as my mum had shown me so the dustbin wouldn't stink, making a cup of tea before work, lying in the bath, steaming up the windows, thinking about what had changed. After three days I got a postcard asking if I was OK.

At work Linda and I hardly looked at each other now. After work, I made my excuses to Pete – I can't even remember how I put him off. He'd guessed something anyway. He'd shrug and smile and put his finger to the side of his nose. Linda had lent me a key, so I could let myself in without half the street knowing. I must have looked surprised, but she'd shrugged as if it wasn't a big deal.

So, it was no surprise to find that Pete had known pretty much everything when we sat up in that hopeless little tent, sipping sour wine from the plastic bottle. We were in Spain, close to the Portuguese border, looking down on the Minho river that we'd have to cross tomorrow. The young guy who served us in the village bar had asked us, *Where you go?* We pointed to the river and beyond. We knew he'd be here forever, working for the family, growing old. I'd watched him and Pete exchange glances. Now Pete slugged the wine, grimacing in a little shudder. *Everyone knew,* he said, *you silly bugger, what did you expect?* What did I expect? I expected everything, but I could never have said what that was. The days were taken by work, but the nights were ours, hot and sleepless, and still somehow unbelievable.

I know I'm supposed to say that one morning I woke and noticed the lines on Linda's face and was overcome by a wave of existential sadness, realising it couldn't last. Or that her ex-husband came to the door one evening and punched my lights out. Or that we failed to connect again after that first time and avoided each other in embarrassment. Or that my parents came home suddenly and found her address on that slip of paper on the kitchen table, putting two and two together. Or how she took me out for one last meal to end it, overcome by bitterness and regret, sipping the last of the wine, envying my freedom when she was tied to work, growing older alone.

But she wasn't tied and none of that happened. Only some of it. It didn't happen because we weren't in a story that had to end with a whimper or a bang or a clever twist of the plot. There wasn't even an ex-husband to turn up. Linda knew when the time was right to end things. Or maybe it was blindingly obvious that we'd only ever have those two weeks. And friendship is so much less destructive than love. The only other person I've ever known who realised that was Pete, who was wise in his own way.

The day before my parents came home we made love for the last time and she stroked my hair as I lay against her and whispered, very simply.

"It's time now, Michael, sweetheart. Thank you."

I lifted my head. I don't know what I'd imagined. I suppose I'd been waiting for this. Dreading it. But maybe it was all there was to say. I felt dazed all the same, kissing her cheek, wanting to cry.

"Thank you. You've been ..."

"I *am*. Just say I am."

She pushed me gently away, her hands lingering on my waist, and I got dressed and went downstairs for the last time, leaving her key on the kitchen table, closing the door, passing the watering can full of peonies that she'd forgotten to water. Suddenly, I felt very small, like a child again.

Then walking home through the dawn chorus. The thin moon about to engulf a star. The house smelled empty and the cat had caught something and was waiting for me, a mouse's tail hanging from its mouth, making that low grizzling noise. The cat set it down, but the mouse was too bewildered to run away. It moved feebly, staring with its shocked eyes until the cat caught it again. I left Marmalade to it and went into the house. Making my bed look slept in. Throwing away the food my mum had left in the fridge. Rumpling the newspapers as if I'd actually read them. Cutting the lawn, watering the window boxes, trying to remember the other dozen things I'd been asked to do.

I never saw Linda again. She was on holiday during my last week at work, then we were packing the car for my first term at Nottingham. Pete knew that something had happened to me, something momentous. But he never asked what it was. Of course, he didn't have to because he already knew. We took up where we'd left off for that last week and he put up with my silences.

I'd lived a lie, for sure, and I felt guilty for reasons that were hard to put in a neat row. I was all over the place. But on one level, things had been simple. Unaccounted. Now they were over, nobody owed anybody anything. What had happened was part of the past, where the present moment had slipped without me ever really noticing until Linda had pushed me gently from the bed.

Then me and Pete again, meeting for a pint after work, watching the cocky young guys from Platts firing back the beer, dancing on the tables at the Sun Mill Inn, cigarettes dangling from their lips. Watching the summer drain away into our futures, the tables strewn with empty glasses in the sinking light. Linda was gone. I knew that was her way of never growing old. *Come on! Come on!* That was Pete, laughing at me from behind his beard, raising a glass of bitter like an ingot. I replied almost without thinking, feeling the pint cool in my hand.

Shoo-be-doo-be-doo-da-day.

Graham Mort

SEPARATED BY
RAIN

I loved you in water
on the gathering side
of a thundercloud
when summer lightning
burnt a silver path
to the hamburger van

from the churn of earth
under my new shoes
to the beauty trickling
down the reflection
on your bus window
rain diluted our leaving

I walked into a goodbye
a stinging downpour
while your hand waved

but it's rain I remember

rain on my numb chin
rain on my forehead
rain and a dented umbrella

all the world dissolved

Robin Lindsay Wilson

STILL

What I love about him
are malting moments in the way
he considers what I've said,
then mashes back with something
surprising. Until him I didn't

relish this liquidity of desire.
Only his teasing is word wort.
I lick the glass with longing.
The edge of his shirt is a border
I traverse slowly, cautiously,

for there are no easy metaphors
though something luxy is lingering
in the washback tracks where a tune
fizzes cupric as he sings to our silence.
Each note stands out like a sett.

Every kiss is grist. Chafing at the spirit
safe the stillman checks our strength.
Casked, our hearts keep steady calm
in the cellared darkness. Taste the air.
Beyond, barley fields sigh lightly.

Briar Wood

NOW WE ARE ALONE
(A MODERN ROMANCE)

Nobody but us to change
the course of this night

and time will never steal
the held breath of now.

We are as intimate
as an open mouth,

ready for the threshold
of yes in our eyes.

I'll be your intrigue
if you'll be mine

and tomorrow
will be another freedom

where I will ask
your name.

Gordon Scapens

THE GREAT ESCAPE

Now I've put out your organic veggies
and watered your mangy cat, Fred,
defrosted the walls of the living-room
and painted the fridge-freezer red...

Now I've shredded your liquorice allsorts,
and made short work of your socks,
wound up your cluttered bedroom drawers
and cleared out your vintage clocks...

Now I've cultivated the milkman
and cancelled that soil for your carrots,
silenced your darts-room radiator
and bled your bleedin' parrots...

Now I've pruned your ship-in-a-bottle
and smashed up your family tree,
taken an axe to your old Apple Mac
and rebooted the wardrobe for me...

I'm determined to freeze every moment
and seize every image for fun
at last, I can bask in the clear blue sky
and reach for the yellow sun!

Doreen Hinchliffe

Under the cover of darkness, a bedraggled figure clicked open the latch of a garden gate and slipped in, unheard through the clamour of the storm. Though his stealthy entrance went unseen and unheard, the crash of the gate behind him as the wind ripped it from his hands must, the young man feared, betray him. He cowered in the darkest spot he could find beneath a dripping lilac tree and watched and listened. Had it been daytime, or had there been even a handful of stars not obscured by the rain-laden clouds and able to shed their feeble glimmer, the light would have revealed his face to be handsome and his black hair to be bedecked with purple petals from the lilac tree. No such light fell and no lights came on in the house. He heard no sounds from the house but he could hardly expect any loud enough to reach him through the howling of the wind.

Once he was satisfied it was safe, he sidled beside the garden wall towards the front door. When he was close he moved across the doorway to get to the narrow path that led to a water butt fed by a drainpipe at the other side of the house. His plan was to climb the drainpipe, which would allow him, with the aid of the virginia creeper higher up, to reach the bedroom window.

He had not thought of the empty bottles put out near the door ready for the early morning visit of the milkman. Too late, he felt his ankle topple the first one. The shrill clatter of what seemed like dozens of bottles colliding and rebounding echoed from the garden walls and made the noise of the storm seem as nothing. He froze again but still detected no movement inside.

Crossing to the overflowing water butt, he pulled himself up until he straddled its rim, put his hands behind the drainpipe, gave it a pull to make sure it was secure, and started to climb. A few feet up he reached out with one foot onto a branch of the virginia creeper, edged higher, brought his other foot over, and continued the climb. Several stems came adrift when he grasped them and reminded him of the precariousness of what he was doing. One time he disturbed a spider or something and it fell off and went down the back of his collar but he was well on his way up the wall and nothing was going to stop him.

When he was within reach of the window he stretched out a hand and tapped on the glass with his finger nails.

Inside the room, the middle-aged occupant, Harold, was already awake. He had almost leapt from his bed when the gate had crashed shut a few minutes earlier. "Drat," he had thought. "I could have sworn I'd closed it properly."

Harold was relaxed and easy going by nature. He liked to think that he could stay calm no matter what he was faced with but there was one thing that made him tense and ill-tempered. He hated windy weather. Most of all he hated banging gates and doors. He tried to rediscover the peaceful sleep that he had been roused from, lying on his back with his hands behind his head, but his heart was still beating like a Harley-Davidson on a fast tick-over.

Just as he was beginning to wander back into a dream there was a cacophony of falling milk bottles.

"Bloody cats!" he screamed, and then added more quietly, as though in apology to an imaginary feline listener, "Oh, sorry. Probably just the wind."

He was well on the way back to sleep when that rattle of finger nails against the window came. There was something going on out there – there must be. He slipped out of bed and walked towards the window but stopped half way. Rather than give away his presence by peering round the curtain he would pad downstairs and out through the front door into the garden to investigate. He suspected he was going to find a ladder with someone either on it or running away from it.

They might not run away: they might be aggressive. He picked up the bedside table lamp to use as a defensive weapon if necessary, unplugged it, and went with it onto the landing. That was when it occurred to him it might not be wise to wander unclothed into the garden, even on a night as dark as this one. So before setting off downstairs he collected a towel from the bathroom and hitched it around himself. He descended the stairs in a haze of something floral that fabric softener had imbued the towel with.

He knew his way around his home well but it was tricky getting from the stairs to the front door and finding the key in the dark. Like the other man earlier, he offered thanks to the noisy weather: it covered the sound of the key turning in the lock and the squeak of the hinge he had been meaning to oil for months. He picked up a torch that he kept near the front door for emergencies such as this (not that there had been any prior emergencies such as this). His bare feet were numbed as he trod in the puddle that formed against the step in wet weather. He went a little further to get a clear view and then turned, switched on the torch, and shone it towards his bedroom window.

He saw no ladder but he saw a frightened youth clinging to the virginia creeper almost at the height of the gutter. The youth did not somehow look like a burglar. Harold had heard about these so-called city night-climbers who did not get enough thrills from climbing on rocks in the daytime and roamed the dark streets looking for adventure. He was not having anybody, young or old, frightened or elated, burglar or harmless crank, scaling his property.

"Get down!" he yelled. "Now!" And he flung his bedside lamp at the intruder.

His aim had never been good and he did not expect to find his target. It did not matter, as long as it unsettled the youth. What happened, however, was certainly not what he intended. The table lamp, missing the youth by several feet, broke straight through the window, became entangled in the curtains, dangled indecisively for several seconds and then fell from view inside the bedroom, leaving just the plug hanging over the window sill.

The youth's response, after having ducked and then straightened up with relief, was to take a precarious swing in the virginia creeper to a position where he could put his head half through the hole in the window, and to shout so loudly that the words, albeit indistinct, reached Harold above the roar of the wind.

"Juliet. Are you all right?"

The youth looked down into the light from Harold's torch and it seemed to remind him that he was a long way from the ground. He started to put together a cry for help but only got out, "Help, I think I'm...," before a stem of the virginia creeper pulled loose. He commenced an ungraceful plummet and landed right in the top of the water butt, his feet and legs up to his knees hooked over one side, his arms and head against the other, and the rest of him immersed.

He let out a gasp at the shock of the cold water. His gasp was not as loud as that of Harold, who was swamped by the wave displaced by the falling body, but the sounds were lost in the bigger and louder splashes and gasps of the rain and wind. There was even some hail starting to batter the two men.

Harold hurried forward, took hold of the young man's hands and hauled him out of the butt. Another couple of gallons of water came out with him and sloshed over Harold's shivering near-naked body. Or rather, over his entirely naked body, as the weight of the water pulled the towel off him while he was helpless to stop it, since both his hands were busy with the rescue.

Harold had dropped his torch, and the two men stood, they supposed, looking into each other's faces, both of them shivering and neither of them less mystified than the other about how they had let themselves come to be where they were.

"Did you shout, 'Juliet'?" Harold asked.

In daylight, the youth's embarrassment would have been evident from the distress in his face and the way he bent his head and kept his eyes on the ground somewhere just in front of where he imagined Harold's feet to be. "I think I must have made a mistake."

"Juliet!" Harold chuckled. "Bad luck, Romeo. Juliet lives next door!"

Neville Judson

THE
COPPERFIELD
DRAUGHT
For the
'Perfidious
Hound of
Canterbury'

This hotel is near another Dickens house.
I can't remember the exact address –
if I could, I'd fail to find it.
The chair fits between
the bed and the desk
(not properly with me on it).
The drawer will open, but
when open won't shut.
Identify the source
without use of devices.

This much of course is for you.
The rest must be shared
with the man we weren't
having lunch with
in Broadstairs.
Sixty-something? Sitting
at the window table.
He wasn't trying
to place us, or at least
I never caught him at it.

Not colleagues, too close
together, and anyway it's Sunday.
Not married – none of that
half-conscious touching,
body language altogether wrong.
Not siblings, no bickering.
And who makes jokes
to their sister
about quite that way
of enjoying Turkish delight?

No, he just sat there,
didn't pretend he wasn't listening
and blessed us. Or that's
what it felt like.

Dear man in the window

This is the woman you were watching.
I liked you too.
Did we look a bit
as if we'd been on the Dickens?
I hope you get this.

Carolyn Oulton

Dream Catcher 41

GROWN argumentative
APART opinions
       but where do you get them from?

       you forgot how to have fun
       you're so full of yourself

       master or victim
       of your domain?

       feel safe
       disregard

       save face
       in your
       safe space

       ego stroked
       (mind states)
       … time
       waits …

       your mild climate migrates
       whilst idly crushing others

       dog smiles
       loyal child
       locked down
       in drown town

       girl cries
       a bird flies
       lost in an ever repeating pattern

       face the water
       taste the wind
       sun sets
       you're dead

       did you ever make anything
       … happen?

       Steve Beadle

THE LODGER

He's no trouble really, been there years
with meals regular and a clean house.
She sees to the washing, irons it all,
does most he asks her, aims to please,
and is always there to say goodbye
when he puts his coat on in the hall.
He doesn't drink much (the sober type)
non-smoker too, so there's never fuss
when lazing both in front of the news
or sharing cocoa at evening's end.
They never argue, she respects his views,
A matter of trust, she tells her friends
and all works out well it seems,
yet quiet in the made-up bed
dwelling in his cold sheet dreams,
he remembers dully a life spent,
long albumed years since they were wed,
sweet vows she swore to him that day,
that two of three were kindly kept,
to honour him and to obey.

Ken Gambles

(1)
As the ambulance, called
fractionally, deliberately, too late,
urges into the traffic, she turns
from the door, aghast,
as the children wake.

(2)
Over the candle flame
a couple melt each other with their eyes
so palpably the other diners,
glancing in embarrassed fascination,
guess they have no bed to go to.
Somewhere else someone finds
a piece of paper in a pocket.

(3)
A country lane. Heat.
A car. Engine running.
Doors open. No one.

(4)
After her stroke her son
does everything for her they say.
Gently, ritually, he washes, lifts, feeds
and whispers, *I hate you.*
I hate you.

(5)
A lodging house.

Alice Harrison

Although she found them rather tiresome, Ursula was obliged to make the return journey back from the cemetery to the funeral parlour with Mr and Mrs Parker. He was tolerable she supposed, although he did have a tendency to think rather highly of himself and had a singular way of trying to catch her eye as if they were on the same wavelength as it were, but she, Mrs Parker, the 'other' grandmother, was wholly unendurable. Unfortunately, the woman occupied the middle seat of the funeral car and so Ursula could not help but take up the seat beside her.

Apparently, the woman was stricken with grief and could not string a sentence together which, Ursula supposed, was one small mercy, but did confirm what she had presumed all along about the weaknesses prevalent in that family. Her in-laws. How she despised that phrase. And she had an innate distrust of those whose emotions were kept close to the surface. Tears on tap, she used to say to Christopher when he was a little boy, all those years ago now. He had very quickly learnt to manage himself properly. Adults who hadn't surpassed that childish phase were to be held in contempt as far as she was concerned. For what was to be done now? Goodness knows one would turn back time if one could, but as that was out of the question, the only way to deal with the situation was to put one's best foot forward, and that was exactly what she said to Christopher at the graveside. He agreed of course, and, after the briefest of wobbles, pulled himself together and began a round of thanks, starting with the vicar. She had looked on approvingly at her grown-up son.

Katherine, on the other hand, headed straight for the undertaker's car which had been assigned to her and Christopher, and, although Ursula could forgive her daughter-in-law for seeking sanctuary at that point, she was inclined to think it another indication of her upbringing. After all, one's guests should be acknowledged, at the very least.

On the way back, in an attempt to lead by example, she waited for a suitable pause in Mrs Parker's hopeless weeping, before remarking upon the tasteful service the vicar had delivered. Mr Parker nodded in agreement and made some doubtful comment about the weather holding up but then found he had nothing more to contribute so Ursula was obliged to fold her gloved hands in her lap and face forwards for the remainder of the journey. The rain slashed against the windows. It was little wonder Katherine had turned out the way she had.

When Ursula had first visited Katherine after the birth, she really did try to make an effort. It was her grandchild after all. And this was despite Katherine's refusal to accept any of her invitations during the pregnancy, claiming sickness or fatigue or some such phantom malady. You wait until the little blighter arrives, she'd thought to herself. Then you'll know tiredness, my dear.

She remembered the ungodly sight of her as she opened the door: hair unkempt, one of those rotting muslin things slung over her shoulder, a pair of trousers that bagged around the bottom. Still in her nightwear, no doubt. The child bawling in the background. Katherine had been rather short with her, quite unlike what Ursula was used to. The girl was usually so careful around her; Ursula got the feeling she didn't want to embarrass herself by saying the wrong thing. Suited Ursula, gave her the upper hand. Always assumed Katherine was following Christopher's lead in showing respect for her elders. But, that morning, Ursula saw a change in her.

'You'd better come in,' Katherine had said. She looked rather fraught and tearful, but it was only a child for heaven's sake and Katherine was often guilty of dramatising the situation. She remembered Christopher relaying Katherine's ultimatum when she'd insisted they move out of the rather unwholesome area of the city they'd found themselves in, ready for the birth of the child. As it happened, she tended to agree with Katherine. After all, one has a responsibility to look after one's own, especially when there are children involved, but it was the manner in which she went about it that she found so distasteful. And Christopher was usually such a loyal boy, but that incident had been beyond even his comprehension and he had told his mother all. It certainly wasn't worth an argument, let alone a separation. Where would the child have been then? Fatherless and forever ashamed of its own mother. Thankfully, because of Christopher, it hadn't come to that, but Ursula filed the incident away as another regrettable aspect of her daughter-in-law's character.

She knew the visit was going to be a brief one when Katherine failed to offer her a cup of tea, but Ursula was not to be deterred. She had come to see her grandson, and see him she would. He was only a few days old, but it was never too early to lay the foundations for success and, judging from her demeanour, Katherine wasn't equipped for the job.

She followed her daughter-in-law into the living room, which was in an unspeakable state of disarray, but held her tongue and peered over the side of the Moses basket in which the child was thrashing about in the manner that newborns often do, and making an unholy racket as he did so.

Quite impulsively, Katherine bent down to pick him up, rocking him on her shoulder, making pointless shushing noises, although, to Ursula, it shouldn't have been that much of a surprise – she might have guessed Katherine would be one of those modern parents who'd have complete disregard for the rule book when it came to routines and boundaries. This was the reason she'd made the journey and seeing Katherine fail so miserably from the very beginning gave her a satisfying sense of justification.

'Can I see the nursery?' she asked. She thought it better to ask questions rather than give direct instructions. She knew from past experience that the girl didn't respond well to being told what to do.

Katherine gave her a puzzled look, and perhaps she imagined it but Ursula thought she detected a touch of insolence in that look, before she slung the defiant child over her other shoulder and led the way upstairs.

From behind, Ursula was able to have an uninterrupted perusal of the child's face. It was vexed, poor thing – needed to be left alone in a dark room – but she could see the irrefutable likeness to Christopher. Eyes spaced a decent way apart and a good, high forehead; the nose and chin would come later. Stubborn too, she could see, and determined. Excellent founding qualities. Just needed to be taken in hand.

Rather than walking her to the spare bedroom – an obvious place for a nursery – Katherine led her into the bedroom she shared with Christopher. Beside the bed, on Katherine's side, sat the cot, like an intruder in the adult world. So, this was where the child slept, and indeed the cot was missing a barred wall, for the side next to the bed was open and the cot pushed close to the mattress so that the baby could come and go as he pleased.

It would hardly do at that point to have suggested the root of Katherine's failure lay in that absurd sleeping arrangement but, needless to say, Ursula disapproved.

Always practical however, she walked over to the windows and drew the curtains closed. Katherine's face had taken on a look of apprehension and she seemed to clutch the child tighter, but she was also trembling with tiredness and was very close to reaching a point where she would find herself entirely without agency. One had to impose one's world on a child; how would they learn otherwise? It would be an unforgivable mistake to allow a child to dictate the course of one's day.

'Come along now,' she said to Katherine, prising the child out of her arms. All Katherine's defiance from their meeting on the doorstep had evaporated and the girl reluctantly relinquished her prize bundle.

Naturally the child broke out into fresh sobs as he arrived in unfamiliar arms and then was placed onto cold, creaseless sheets.

'He's used to the Moses basket in the day,' Katherine said uselessly as Ursula ushered her out of the room.

'Nonsense,' she replied, propelling her downstairs and into the kitchen. 'The child doesn't know the difference between night and day.'

Ursula herself filled the kettle and found the teabags, which would have to do in lieu of anything decent. The girl was fretting and wouldn't settle, rather like her untamed child, but this wasn't the time for a good talking to. Instead, Ursula handed her a cup of tea and led her to a chair. On the way to the kitchen, she'd closed each door behind them so the child's outraged cries were muffled somewhat, but Katherine still flinched every time it howled anew.

'After your tea, why don't you have a little stroll?' Ursula suggested. She wasn't a monster; she knew how difficult this was for Katherine to sit through. The child wouldn't take long to settle but every second was an interminable one for the girl and it would be best if she could distract herself with something rather than torture herself listening to it kick up a fuss. And she knew from experience the screams would get louder before they quietened completely. It would be best if she weren't around to hear that.

'I couldn't leave him,' she said.

'I think it best,' was her simple reply. The girl had tired herself out and had nothing left in her reserves. Ursula found her coat and gave her a reassuring smile as she opened the front door. A pleasant day: warming up after the winter. Later on, Katherine could lay the baby in the pram, wrap it in blankets, turn its face to the sun. She used to do something similar with Christopher whilst she planted up the vegetable beds for early potatoes.

'Why don't you walk to the shops and pick yourself up something for dinner? Christopher could do with a hot meal when he comes in from work.'

It did the trick. The mention of Christopher and the suggestion she wasn't keeping up with the tight day-to-day operation that a family needs caused a new line of worry to appear on Katherine's forehead. She really was at her lowest. Ursula closed the door behind her and went back to the kitchen where she threw the tea down the sink and settled herself in for the battle.

Back at the funeral parlour she said a polite but terse goodbye to the Parkers. It was important to remain civil with these people, but there was no need to pretend they had anything in common. Mrs Parker didn't seem to hear her and instead dashed over to Katherine, who was being led by Christopher from the undertaker's car to their own, and threw herself on her daughter. Poor Christopher, she thought, as she watched him try to remove the woman from his wife. Thankfully, Mrs Parker allowed herself to be prised off but then transferred her lamentations onto Christopher. That suit will need a thorough dry cleaning, Ursula thought to herself, as she looked on. What a dreadful woman. One must respect the formalities around death and making such undignified demonstrations was no help to anyone.

She would leave them in peace, as she had assured Christopher at the church. He didn't need to ask; the etiquette around funerals was something she was more than familiar with. When Kenneth died, the last thing she wanted was people turning up on her doorstep with casseroles. It wasn't as if she'd lost all ability to function, in fact, continuing with one's routines – meals at set times, tuning in for the 6 o'clock news and so on – was necessary to getting back on one's feet. No sense in moping around.

Naturally, she'd had to send her apologies to various meetings and charity functions for a couple of weeks after the funeral, but when the proper period of mourning was over she had returned to social life with gusto. It was what Kenneth would have wanted and, more importantly, it was what she needed. In no time at all she was up and running again. It wasn't that she didn't think about him from time to time, of course she did, but he wasn't coming back and so she set her mind firmly to the future: the only direction of travel was forward.

She was confident Christopher had learnt enough from her example to do the same, although the death of a child was quite a different matter to the death of a spouse, or in Christopher's case, a father, who had lived a long and fulfilled life. Christopher's recovery would not be without its difficulties, but if he were to survive this episode, he would need to do as she had done.

Her worry was with the girl, who had not grown up with the best role models and, Ursula was guessing, did not have the resources to cope with such a significant loss. She would do what she could for her, but, for now, she would take a step back.

Turning away from her son, who by now had successfully managed to get his wife into the passenger seat, Ursula was surprised to feel what could only be described as an emotional tug. A frightful expression, but it came to her without warning. She supposed she could allow such a slippage on a day like today. After all, one cannot help but imagine oneself in the position of the bereaved at a funeral. And she was not without affection for her grandson. Charles, although only a boy, had still had the potential to grow into a fine young man; she had not lost all hope by the time he died. Despite the obvious influence of the boy's mother, there had still been time to rectify some of her mistakes and Ursula had recently been spending more time with him in order to do just that.

He'd become a rather delicate child, long, thin limbs like his father, but with no substance to them. Ursula had also had the occasion to observe, in recent months, that the boy would cling to his mother whenever she delivered him to her door. His mother would do very little to discourage this unfortunate behaviour so that Ursula was often obliged to be sharp with him in order to get him indoors. Never one to make a fuss, she would forbid him from sitting at the window to wave goodbye to his mother and tell him to eat his biscuit and drink his milk before sending him out the back door to get some much-needed fresh air. A couple of hours rambling over fields and scratching his knees on brambles ought to toughen him up, she'd thought, but after twenty minutes or so had found him within the walls of the yard where she keeps the fowl, stroking the rather perplexed chickens.

Five years old is a formative time in a young boy's life; the memory of Christopher at the same age was still rather vivid. She well remembered how she'd spent two years preparing him for boarding school so that when he was sent off at seven, he was more than equipped not only to survive but also to do rather well and she was proud of the work she had done. She had hoped to do something similar for Charles, but it wasn't to be. Opening her car door, she dismissed the thought and managed to drive steadily off in her reliable Land Rover.

That afternoon she had an engagement to keep – a late golfing luncheon – and she would need to go straight there if she were to be prompt. The invitation had been sent months ago, as these things often are to ensure a decent turnout, and she had accepted. As a general rule, she accepted any social event with a high profile and the promise of an interesting speaker. However, the events of the past two weeks being what they were, she had realised three days ago that the date clashed, and had half thought of withdrawing her acceptance, but no, she had decided, she would attend, for wasn't this exactly what she had been urging Christopher to do. One had to carry on.

Holly Sykes

In practical terms, it's easier meeting someone at Leeds airport than somewhere like Heathrow. Arrivals come through in a trickle by comparison – in single file a lot of the time. But you feel more exposed, recognising the person you are waiting for and doing the greetings and stuff, with just a handful of strangers looking on. A heedless crowd would be better.

I don't remember a lot about my early childhood in Zimbabwe. Well, Rhodesia actually – it was Rhodesia then. I have a hazy memory of sitting on the veranda watching a thunder storm, huge raindrops splashing onto the ground a metre away and sending warm spray onto us. The maid was sitting with us and she kept laughing at the things my parents were saying. We had several servants – I'm not sure how many, but there was her and a cook who lived in, somebody who came in a few days a week and a gardener who did not live with us but seemed to be around most of the time.

The maid – Comfort, she was called – was like part of the family to me, being there so much and being so intimate with my parents – especially my father. Then she walked out one afternoon and never visited us again. My parents never mentioned her. The nearest they came to it was when we went for a picnic by a lake in the Rhodes Matopos National Park near where we lived in Bulawayo.

My father was gazing across the water and, without turning to her, he said to mother, "I suppose we ought to get another maid."

"There's no sense in spending the money," my mother said. "I can manage perfectly well." She was looking steadfastly at the hills across the lake, too.

When we came back to England we settled on the edge of London. We had to live there, with my father working at the Foreign Office and my mother joining the BBC as a journalist. We could not afford servants any more, apart from a cleaner who came in a couple of times a week, but we had a rather grand house in Virginia Water.

For most of my early life, I thought my parents were the perfectly matched couple. Never once were voices raised between them. Maybe they were so much in agreement with each other that they had no cause to argue but I realise now that they would hardly have known if they were in agreement or not. They did not talk about anything – not anything of consequence, I mean. They chatted away all the time but it was never about themselves. They talked about the weather, the hedgehog that visited our garden in the evenings, what the cat had brought home, how Mrs Spencer up the road was going on with her disabled husband, but never about their own needs and feelings.

It was as though they wanted to be together but something kept them at a distance. I thought it was old-fashioned reserve and I was shocked when I discovered it was the shared denial of a secret that pushed them apart, like the same poles on two magnets. Perhaps father had dug himself in so far that he was too ashamed to talk about it. I think mother had stopped caring – she just wanted him to sort himself out and tell the truth.

It was a benign drifting apart. No rows, no bitterness – there just came a time when they saw no point in staying together. Coldness does not engender fireworks; it just eats away at the ties between people. By then I had married, moved to Leeds, and had a son, Christopher. He would have been ten, I think. I went down to London to help them with sorting out their things when they cleared the house, and took Christopher with me. They were moving into separate small flats and a lot of the things in the house would have to go. They had said I could have whatever I wanted. It would only end up on the tip otherwise.

I had filled a box with clothes out of the attic that might come in useful and sent Christopher downstairs with it, and I was going through a pile of books, when mother called up to me. "What have you done with my diamond brooch?"

She was in the master bedroom one floor below me.

"I haven't done anything with it. It's on the dressing table in your room – at least it was half an hour ago."

"No, it isn't. I'm there now."

"Perhaps father has put it in one of his boxes."

"Don't be ridiculous. What would *he* want it for?"

It struck me there was something in her voice that conveyed, unsaid, 'As if it isn't obvious what he would want it for.'

Anyway, we both went downstairs to father and Christopher, where father was moving boxes about in the hallway to make room for more. "You haven't got my diamond brooch in your things, have you, Ben?" Mother asked.

"Of course I haven't." He turned to me. "Have you packed it, Eileen? It would be just like you to stow something like that away without asking first."

I was outraged. As I saw it, they had both as good as accused me of stealing the thing. I did not even like it much. It was too old-fashioned.

"This is the only box I've put anything in so far," I said, going over to the one Christopher had brought downstairs. "Look for yourself."

I lifted the lid and there, lying on top of the clothes, was the brooch. For a second I was mystified but then I noticed Christopher looking sheepish.

"You put it in there, didn't you, Christopher? What did you do that for? I told you not to interfere."

"I want you to have it. If granddad gets it he'll give it to Felicia."

"What are you talking about? Granddad does not know anybody called Felicia, does he?" I said, looking to father for an answer.

Christopher continued. "Yes, he does. He's got lots of Western Union forms in his desk drawer and they all have 'Felicia' written on them. I saw them when he let me go to work with him. I expect he's got a lover so he won't be lonely now granny's leaving him, so that's all right, but I want mummy to have the brooch, not Felicia."

"Christopher! ..." I started, but father held up his hand.

"You remember Comfort? The maid we had in Rhodesia who left when she got pregnant."

Mother said. "She didn't leave. I sacked her. I've felt bad about how we treated that woman all the rest of my life. She didn't deserve to be abandoned." She turned to me. "Why else does he think I've gone along with his stories about losing money on the horses? It was obvious he was sending it to her. Much as I wanted to believe he was just doing the honourable thing, the way his supposed gambling losses got bigger and bigger, he was either a lot closer to Comfort than he admitted or else he was being blackmailed. In the end, it didn't matter which it was. I despised him for it either way."

Father half shook his head and said, "I sent her a bit of money after we came back to London but she did not live long – malaria, or some disease they assumed to be malaria. I carried on sending money for the child. I've never said. It seemed better not to." He pulled a photograph out of his pocket. "This is Felicia. It was hard to do when she got older – drawing enough from the bank account to pay for her to go to university..."

Mother and father took themselves off into the kitchen and we stayed where we were, not sure what we were supposed to do. When they eventually came back, they told us they were going to give it another week or two. The years rolled on but they never separated.

Father died a couple of years ago. Mother is frail now and does not come to see me in Leeds any more. I go down to London as often as I can. My half-sister has wanted to meet me for a long time and in the end I agreed to send her a formal invitation and she got her visa. Mother wants to see her while she is here. I am not sure whether to arrange that or not. All I know right now is that I should like to turn and run away. I am scared about how I might react in front of these strangers when Felicia comes through.

The arrival doors slide open. Here she is. Very smart. Very black – you can't be sure from photographs – I had expected her to look mixed race. Smiling. Looking straight at me. She lets go of her suitcase and steps forward, her arms outspread.

Neville Judson

Dylan Thomas, poet

I KNOW THE THOUGHTS THAT SURROUND YOU

I've never forgotten that old pop song
you cradled in your record collection.
I could never stand it but its presence
made you human, when on weekdays you talked like Che Guevara
and weekends you danced like Ian Curtis.

You've still got the talk, when the camera pins you
and your mask twinges, animatronic, round the corners of your mouth.
The dance, too, when the image sours into guilt.
You still swill your cans of cheap cider
but you never get your lips wet.

I've stayed behind that library desk,
memorised the Dewey Decimal System.
You've memorised your spin doctor's candyfloss language
but can't remember just who you are.

But where do you go to, my lovely
when you're alone in your bed?
I hope it's the Channel Tunnel
where there are people locked in by your hand.
Now you'll never get to the Boulevard St. Michel
because you'd have to look into their faces.
You don't want to catch anything. No you don't.

As for the song,
one day you'll pick it for Desert Island Discs.
That'll be the human thing to do.

Poppy Bristow

ALICE'S HAIR

In 1943, Alice, my grandmother's nurse
asked if an American GI she knew should
photograph her wearing nothing but her hair,
which, unpinned, was longer than a sermon.
And Alice's hair was a Sunday dress.

With shaking hands smoothing creases
Alice added, I know what you'll say
but the thing is, the thing is
we could all be dead tomorrow.
And Alice's hair was the last thread.

My grandmother was surprised,
but saw what they both saw;
Alice's breasts and thighs the waves in a sea of hair
carrying Humphrey Bogart into battle.
And Alice's hair was the South Pacific.

He's not normally one for this sort of thing,
Alice was at pains to explain.
At home he paints sets for the movies.
And Alice's hair lit up Sunset Boulevard.

There were so many ladders in
my grandmother's stockings that
she used to say at least we'll have
something to climb out the windows with
if the Japs bomb us.
But Alice had nylons now.
And Alice's hair was a parachute escape.

My grandmother touched her submarine belly.
Alice, do you really, do you really think . . .
but she didn't know what she thought herself.
And Alice's hair swaddled my mother.

Finally she managed,
If you were my daughter, I'd say . . .
But the baby kicked before she could finish.
Alice just looked out the window.
And Alice's hair trailed behind the steamer,
the smoke that would take her over the ocean
to light Clark Gable's cigarette.

Kathryn Haworth

THE PEOPLE WHO LIVE INSIDE ME

She often said, my mother,
That's not for the likes of you
and she goes on saying it
even though she's dead,

and my father, when I crashed
his car, said over and over
Bugger the car, are you all right?

Other voices keep butting in:

Don't screw up your face like that,
a changing wind makes it permanent
and no-one will want to marry you.

Tread on a nick and you'll marry a brick
Tread on a square and you'll marry a bear.

You won't get into the house, love.
Your mum's run off with a tramp.

And the mesh of the voices that bothered me
blends with what I thought I heard my parents
say in bed on the darkest nights
that puzzled and frightened me

and knits together with all the other words
inside the head of a child who's a grandmother now
yet even more of a child, bewildered,
still trying to learn the impossible language.

Jean Stevens

WHEN YOU LET ME GO

You left me a shiny black shoe,
its tongue lolling on one side,
clothes splayed on my bed
like tarot cards.

You left me a hand-made coat
fluttering moons and stars
to touch the sky, you said,
with an odd number of buttons,
if eleven it will be fine.

You left an opened book by the window,
pages flapping on the desk,
a letter ripped between your name
and surname. I remember your writing,
its arrhythmic rifts and dips, its hanging loops.

I remember blushing
as we shopped for my first
bra with baby blue cups,
you, unable to tell me the facts of life,
you, unable to fasten the hooks.

I remember how you always shut
your eyes when I said *no*
as if resisting a kiss, all the kisses
I hold on to now that you've let me go.

María Castro Domínguez

THE WINES OF MY FATHER
in memory of Peter C. Tracy 1917 - 1988

Strawberry picking days in Cheddar,
lemons from the Mediterranean,
summer distilled into bottles.
Dandelions collected at eleven o'clock
from the sunny field by the brook
don't bring expected tastes of gold and sunshine.
Peapod leaves the throat numb;
my father drinks the bottle,
against my mother's scoffing,
to prove it alcoholic,
watches Botham bowl double balls down the wicket;
we laugh until he sleeps it off
and pour the others down the drain.
The sloes are only for gin
in the brown paper bag behind the TV,
ritually shaken morning and evening.

When I visit from university,
we drive to his friend Alec's cellar,
retrieve a couple of bottles,
sample Alec's latest wine too early;
my father secretly prefers its sweetness.
Superior in my zealous new ideals,
after the celebratory meal
we argue with passion, and finally with rage –
my mother always blames his wine.

A hundred years after his birth,
thirty years after his death,
I've reached his winemaking years;
we could share a glass of strawberry or lemon,
(steering clear of the pea pod),
maybe sigh over lost liberal values,
and find a little less to argue about.

Heather Deckner

RELIC

Easter, and I'm crossing the Cleveland Hills,
Losing My Religion full on through the sun roof

as you stow the relics of a dead husband
in your attic, filling a tall house
with withered climbing gear,

a grounded kayak I later help you free.
Picture us down at the quayside, posing
by the whale bones, the Abbey's silhouette.

Thirty years on and you're not
anymore. I'm losing my religion.

Jenny Hockey

Graves seem even more grim in the cold and sleet.
That place chills us to the bone,
It's very smell staying with us for days,
reminding us we are just tiny pawns in the big game,
with our backs against the wind,
shivering against the day
flowers are placed with love,
but they keep blowing over
petals drifting like confetti;
his face tells me he's wishing,
pleading her spirit,
their sweet lady of ladies as he calls her,
is somewhere more deserving
than in the cold hard ground
with so many forgotten names;
I grab his hand and hold it tight.
The spark of warmth makes him sigh.

Deborah Maudlin

TWO LETTERS

Unsent

I want to tell you as you sit in this one room
that the London Streets you left are just the same.
The city square you loved is inscribed
with green traces and magnolia blossom.
The railings outside the school where you taught
still bounces with children.

The light here floods in from the distant view
and you remember your mother's evening dresses,
your father's terrible jokes and jaunty smile.
This is your come and go: all that happened before.
So I won't say bedridden or house-bound but
rather the woman who can laugh when I read
her John Betjeman. Who has lost all time,
and refuses to let it grow shabby in her heart.

Winter Letters

They were still in their envelopes,
where I put them into dust and dark.
They seemed imprinted with the day
they were written, frank of a postage
stamp, ink blurring an old address.
I thought of you walking down a darkened street.
Posting them, leaving the desk where you wrote.
The heft of our feelings textured in sentences.
They would arrive on frost cold mornings,
lie on the mat. Only tearing or burning
would delete your ghost shape.
Part of us folded between the pages,
like calligraphy as we talked
across distances in a slow hand.

Clare Crossman

Forty years ago, in the depths of a Nordic winter, I got spooked.

I'd wake up in cold sweats, thinking that a pack of wolves were after me, chasing me through the Arctic snow, baring their teeth, out for blood. Night after night, week after week, the same nightmare. A horror show that seemed to have no end. It got to the point where I feared the night, where I was even afraid of going to sleep. You could say I was afraid of my own shadow.

Why? Turn back the clock to 1977. My dad had been offered a job abroad working on oil rigs, so the family had moved to Norway, to an island called Stord. He was an oil man and proud, with his yellow hard hat, faded jeans and steel toe-capped boots, working long shifts on the concrete pillars they built for oil platforms.

On Stord we lived near Leirvik, in an old wooden house called Knutsehuse. Painted all in white, set in woodland high up on a hill looking out over the North Sea, the house came complete with stables and a lake that teemed in summer with trout and frogs and dragonflies. It was like a rabbit warren inside. We all had our own rooms. There was always something new to discover in its maze of corridors, bedrooms and bathrooms. We read ghost stories late at night, then crept around the house with a torch in the early hours, searching for the great unknown. It was a magical place, steeped in history, with Nordic memories emanating from every corner.

Summers were very mild, hot even. The locals celebrated Norwegian Constitution Day on the seventeenth of May in a blaze of sunshine and colour. But winters were very, very cold. So cold you dared not open the window at night. Dad used to tell us that if you did, you wouldn't wake up in the morning. He said that Norway could get colder than Canada in winter, with the temperature sometimes dropping to minus twenty or worse at night. And then there was the snow. Entire frozen miles and miles of snow.

You had to learn to love the snow. Beautiful yet deadly, it was something you had to learn to work to your advantage. We put on our gloves and jackets and snow boots and built igloos in the back garden with ice bricks made from packing snow into an old plastic bucket. One winter we built two igloos, one so big that Dad could stand up in it, and a smaller one that was like an annexe, connected to the main one by a long ice tunnel.

One evening, as the snow abated and the sun set over the bay, we were all having dinner when there was a quiet knock at the door. First we all just sat there, thinking it was the wind, but then it came again. A quiet, persistent knock. I got up from the table, raced down the corridor and opened the front door. Standing there was a boy a few years older than me, my elder brother's friend from school. He looked terrified, he looked like he'd seen a ghost. My brother got up from the table and joined me at the door as the boy told us that there was someone hanging around in the stables down the drive. Some strange old man. Dad went and fetched a torch and we put on our coats and boots and crept down the driveway in the snow.

When we reached the stables, all was quiet there apart from the sound of the horses who stood there in the night. They breathed the freezing cold air and their eyes shone like black pearls in the moonlight. They seemed calm enough, so we moved on to the next stable, expecting it to be empty. But lying there in the hay was an old man with a red beard flecked with grey, a bottle of whisky by his side. It made me shiver, seeing him there. He seemed oblivious to our presence as he muttered to himself in Norwegian. Dad said it was best just to leave him to his own devices. Let sleeping dogs lie, that's what he said. He wasn't doing anyone any harm. So we went back up to the house and I went to bed.

But the trip down to the stables had spooked me more than I thought and it was then that the wolf nightmares began. I did my best to forget about them, but they never went away.

It seemed as though we were on a constant search for adventure. Dad took us skiing at every opportunity. We packed our bags and left the house with the Range Rover loaded up with skis and poles and wax and boots and then we were off on another skiing holiday.

We took the ferry from Stord to the mainland and drove for hours up into the mountains north of Bergen, until the snow was twenty feet high on either side. Then Dad got out and put the snow chains on the wheels and we crawled up a mountain track until we got to a chalet with a sauna and bunk beds and heated floors.

The next morning we were up early. The sun was just climbing over the horizon as we ate our breakfast and prepared our skis. This wasn't slalom skiing with the fancy boots and the wide skis and the ski lifts which took all the effort out of it. This was langlauf.

We headed out from the chalet, down the hill, falling over again and again on our narrow old-fashioned skis. Dad was the expert. Or at least he thought he was. He'd learned a lot from his Norwegian friends, at any rate. First you had to get the wax right, that's what he said. You had to put enough wax on the bottom of the skis or they would stick on the snow. Once you got that right, it was all technique. It was all about keeping the skis parallel and relaxing in your ski boots and bending your knees. Once you got the knack, you were skiing on air.

We glided down the hill in a winter ballet with our ski poles tucked under our arms and our hats pulled down over our ears. When we finally reached the bottom of the hill, then came the climb. We placed our skis at a diagonal and marched up the hill through the snow, one ski over the other. Once we got into a rhythm, we bounced up the hill like snow hounds.

At the top of the hill we gathered together and looked out over the mountain scape beyond. Most of it was untouched, virgin snow that sparkled and shone in the winter light. And it was all so quiet. As though the snow absorbed all sound. A flat plain of snow stretched out about a mile to the east. It was pancake flat and I thought it looked strange surrounded by the snow-clad hills. It shone purple and blue in the ultraviolet sun. I asked Dad what it was and he told me it was a lake, frozen solid with a layer of snow over the top. We stood there as a family for a long time, taking it all in, looking out over the lake and the snowscape, hypnotized by the ultraviolet light and by the silence on the hill.

Dad took off his rucksack and put it down in the snow. He pulled out a thermos flask, removed the metal lid and unscrewed the thermos. He poured some coffee into the lid and drank the whole thing. He refilled it and passed it round, urging each of us to take a sip.

"We're going to head down there now, guys. Get this down you before we move on again. Keep your wits about you."

We all took a glug and he put the thermos flask back together and placed it back in his rucksack. He swung the rucksack over his shoulders and then he was off down the hill like a demon, a winter demon careering through the snow. His body swerved left and right in a smooth rhythm until he banked hard left, skidded around on his skis and stopped by the side of the lake.

He turned round and looked back up the hill, beaming at us through his goggles and the white sunblock on his face. He called out to us to ski down the hill and join him.

We headed off down the hill in turn, first of all my sister, then myself and my two brothers, and finally my mother. It wasn't steep. One by one we joined him down at the bottom of the hill by the lake. And he looked out over its surface, over to the outline of a village on the far side. The sun was high in the sky now. It must have been about midday.

"That's the village we're headed for. Should only take us half an hour to get there now."

I looked out across the lake. There was fresh snow on its surface but there were still faint tracks in the snow from where people had skied across. Dad turned back towards the lake and pushed himself out over the snow and ice. He stopped for a moment and lifted one of his ski poles and thrust it firmly into the snow on his left. Then he pulled the ski pole out again and repeated the action until he was satisfied. He turned back to us and grinned.

"Frozen solid. Like concrete. Come on guys, let's get moving! Lunch in half an hour!"

We stood there by the lakeside, breathing heavily, our breath visible in the cold air. If there was any fear among us, it didn't show. We had skied across frozen lakes before. We were used to it by now.

Dad skied out across the lake and we all followed in turn. Skiing almost in single file, following the tracks that were already there in the snow, we made quick progress across the wide expanse of the frozen lake. From time to time my sister looked back and grinned at us. I smiled back at her and then did the same, turning to look back at the others as they made their own way across the ice.

At one point my elder brother glanced off to the left and spotted another set of tracks in the snow, parallel to our own. Curiosity got the better of him and he veered off to the left and was suddenly skiing alongside the rest of us, a couple of metres away. Dad scowled at him and told him to stop horsing around, to come back and rejoin the rest of the family. But my brother just ignored him and quickened his pace. And soon he was ahead of us, pushing on without a care in the world. We ignored him and continued to make our own way across the lake.

And just as we were nearly across, everything changed. Where one moment we were all cruising across the ice and my brother was up ahead, skiing along in the new tracks in a dream world of his own, the next moment suddenly he was gone. A scream from my mother echoed across the snow and the ice.

We all stopped dead in our tracks. I looked up as a feeling of terror shot through my body like raw electricity. And all I saw off in the distance was my brother's head poking out through a hole in the ice, through a wide hole that had suddenly opened up in the lake from nowhere. What happened next was a blur. Dad turned back and called out.

"Stop here! Don't go any further!"

Then he turned ahead again and skied off towards my brother. When he was near him, he snapped off his skis and took careful steps towards the hole in the ice. He crouched down and lay down on his belly and slid himself the rest of the way. As he did so, a crack appeared at the edge of the ice hole and continued to grow off to his left. He took one look at it and the blood just drained from his face. For a moment he did nothing. Then he slid himself off to the right, away from the crack, and moved himself away from the ice hole. He got up and marched back towards us.

"Quick! Give me your poles!! Give me all your ski poles!!"

We did as we were told. As I skied up to him, I looked down, half expecting the ice to give way under my skis. But it was still solid here. We all handed our ski poles to him and he acted without thinking, driven by pure instinct, tying the ski poles together into a long line with their straps. He called out as he worked.

"Vincent!!"

There was no response. He called out again as he continued working with the ski poles.

"Vincent! Vincent, talk to me!!"

My brother was still up ahead, his head just above the ice. He had an arm out of the water now and he was clutching at the edge of the ice. As he clutched at it, a large chunk of ice broke off from the edge, making the hole in the ice even bigger. Dad looked up.

"Forget it! I'm going to throw this line to you! OK?"

No response.

"I'm going to throw you the ski poles and you're going to grab hold of them. You got that?"

My brother called out to confirm. Dad didn't want to venture any closer, in case the ice cracked again and he went in too. He gathered the ski pole line together and flung it out towards my brother, who was still treading water in the murky lake. My brother lunged at it but missed. The ski poles went clattering across the ice. Dad cursed under his breath and hauled them back towards him and gathered the line back together.

"Again!"

He flung the poles out to my brother again, and once again he lunged for it, grabbing hold of the line briefly, but it slipped out of his hands. Once again Dad hauled the poles back and gathered the line together.

"We're running out of options here! Just grab hold of the line!"

He flung the poles out again, and this time my brother lunged out of the water and grabbed the line with both hands.

"OK, you got it?"

"Yep."

"OK, I'm going to pull it taut so don't let go."

My brother nodded. He was weak but he was a fighter and he was holding on for dear life. Dad pulled on the other end until it was taut. Then he turned round and dug his boots into the snow and the ice.

"Right, I'm going to drag you out of there. So hold on tight! OK?"

Again the confirmation from my brother. Dad took firm steps across the lake. He didn't look back. All his energy was focused on stepping forwards, dragging the ski pole line behind him. He just carried on and on, until my brother was hauled like a porpoise out of the water and onto the solid ice of the lake. Still Dad did not look back. He just kept stepping forwards across the ice. He called out again.

"You still holding on to those poles?"

"Yes, Dad. Yes. I'm OK. You can stop now."

Dad stopped in his tracks and dropped the line. He walked back towards my brother, who lay there shivering and shaking on the ice. He called over to the rest of us, as we huddled there in shock on the frozen expanse of the lake.

"I'm going to carry Vincent! Come and get your poles and get yourselves off the lake and to the village! And take my skis as well!"

As he said this, he took off his ski jacket and wrapped it round my brother. Then he picked him up and put his shivering body over his shoulder. We took the ski pole line apart, shared the poles amongst us and skied off the lake. Minutes later we were sitting on a bench on the other side of the lake, watching as Dad trudged across the lake with my brother.

Then we all headed for the nearest inn, where we rented a couple of rooms and camped down for the night. My mother tended to my brother, peeling off his sodden clothes, towelling him dry. Then she wrapped him in blankets and sat him in front of the fire until the shivers went away.

That night I had another nightmare, this time that we were all skiing across the ice again. Suddenly the ice gave way and an enormous sea creature, a leviathan, rose up out of the ice with impossible energy. We stood there as it opened its monster jaws, swallowed the entire family, then plunged down into the water again, its body sending a wave of snow and ice and water across the lake like a winter tsunami.

As I had done before, I woke up in a cold sweat. I looked across the bedroom in the moonlight, at my brothers lying there in bed, fast asleep. I watched them there for a long time, their breathing slow and steady and tranquil, interrupted with the occasional snore and the occasional shuffle, as they slept on into the night. And then I looked out of the window, at the lake which reflected the moonlight back into the room. At the snow and the ice, beautiful, magical and deadly.

And as I lay there, reminiscing about the events of the day, my nightmares were suddenly of no consequence at all. The Arctic wolves and the sea monster were now rendered obsolete, caricatures of what they had been. I lay back down in bed and listened to the sounds of the night.

Paul Saville

Boundaries fascinate. There is an atunement between curiosity and the edges of things. The edge of the horizon is perhaps the clearest case, but there are many others. The line of mountain against sky, or the line where atmosphere becomes the vacuum of space, or the border between sleep and waking. The highly curious always become boundary-chasers in one way or another.

The black gleaming cosmic nothingness of the Arctic Ocean lapped the snow. It would slip its tongue up, run it over the white, and then slide it back into its immense maw. The snow remained, impervious. More of it was falling through the shipyard lights as she stood and watched the boundary between the sea and Spitsbergen. She thought about how that same black water lay under the ice of the North Pole, not all that far away. Seeing how calm the lapping of the sea was here made this easier to imagine. She could imagine cutting a bore hole into sea ice and coming face to face with this same gleaming mass. A completely different entity to the salt grey oceans of crashing waves and foam, this was more brooding, sentient. A gust of wind forced Julia to pull her hood over her head and duck under the shelter of the fur trim. She turned her back on the ocean, with a prickle of adrenaline as if she had turned her back on a predator, and began to walk back towards town. The icy patches on the road shone like mirrors in the street light, and gusts of wind would send snow dust snaking over them in long sweeping patterns.

An arctic fox will travel persistently over the landscape, leaving its little patters of footprints across the vastness of the snow. A small white creature, perfectly camouflaged, just trotting always onwards along the peripheries of some unseen territory. Julia saw the tracks, but never the animal, though she always carried ham stolen from the breakfast buffet in her pocket just in case. She associated with the fox, with its constant movement. Her aim had always been to keep moving, and to never become pinned down. She feared attachment like a trapper's snare. But then, she had finally crossed paths with someone who had pinned her securely to himself, and now she couldn't roam away. She knew that coming to the arctic was part of pulling against the bond, and testing herself to see how much of the tearing pain she could take. She was looking for the edge here too, finding the rim of how far away her love would permit her to stray. The arctic fox trails soothed some of the worry she carried about this attachment. These foxes mated for life, after all. And yet here were all these travels in the snow, countless footfalls on an endless roaming journey.

Her walks always took her to the limits of town, which was not surprising given how small the inhabited nook of the island was. The valley walls cut a thin, austere space for houses and roads, cordoned off from the snowy desert. At the mouth of the valley the ocean marked the end of her walks, and inland they stopped where the street lights ceased along with the road, and ahead there was nothing but the deep unending night, and even deeper snow. The discomforting thing about deserts, she thought, was their sheer scope. If she were to walk out into the snowy wastes, she would always be in the desert's centre, always moving towards the horizon but never able to reach it and lean over its precipice. Julia picked a road at random, winding up the valley side, and walked it until it came to a final house. A light was on, showing a wooden interior, decorated with sprigs of evergreen, stocky candles, embroidered cushions. Clearly no one was inside. She tried the door, and it opened. No one locked anything in this town. Warm interior air brushed her face, dry and sweet. She looked at the hallway, with coats and boots, a mirror with crayon drawings tacked to it. She considered going inside, and looking at the things that marked these people's life here. She looked at the threshold of the house, but the will to cross it wasn't in her today. She was just treading the line. She shut the door and turned away. Ahead of her the darkness remained impermeable. She stood, and stared out, seeing nothing, for a long time.

For New Year's Eve Julia obeyed a tradition from her childhood, which she liked even though she usually abhorred ritual of any kind. She would make an offering of flowers to the ocean goddess. She didn't expect a reward, no wish making or luck, as she knew better than to ask the mercurial waters for anything they weren't already going to give. She just liked to be at the water when the year turned, and to give the flowers to the waves. There were no flowers in the polar winter, so she sat in the coffee shop in the afternoon making origami lotuses and lilies. People would glance at her, but their boundaried Norwegian nature wouldn't permit them to stare, or ask her why she was making paper flowers. She liked this culture of privacy. She thought again of the house with the unlocked door, and how easy it would be to slip into people's spaces and examine them in this town, where there is no crime, where there is no instinct to cross into other people's worlds.

She walked to the end of the road, and then through a deep snow bank that came up her thighs with a tight grip when she sank in. Then she slowly, tentatively slid over the ice, past a line of parked busses, to the water. She had chosen the spot because there were no bright lights, so the ocean was truly omnipresent in the night. She stood with her boots on the wet pebbles, letting the waves wash over their rubber toes. She gazed out ahead into the perfect darkness. She knew there were mountains on the other side of the narrow strait, but without moonlight there was nothing ahead at all. There was nothing inside her either. Julia was only blank space marked out by the outlines of everything around her. She herself was empty, just like the polar night. Here, at the water's edge, there was very little left around her to form her boundary. She felt it dissolving away, letting her own empty space bleed into all the other emptiness, till she would cease to be distinguished from it. Her existence wavered in the dark. Julia took a few steps into the water, feeling her outline vibrate, loosen. The water rose over the waterproof base of her boots, and began to seep in through the upper fabric. It cut her feet like razor blades. The cold pain sent a shock of longing through her body. It was painful the way being away from her lover was painful, like the tugging of him in the distance. She stared at the black mass of the water, and felt that she didn't belong to it. She belonged elsewhere, with her mate. She opened her bag, and pulled out her paper flowers, and with her hands shaking from the cold she scattered them into the water. She gave the flowers instead of herself, and watched them drift over the boundary of visibility into the void. She turned, and walked back into the snow, shaking and breathing hard from the frosty pain. In front of her, flares went up, luminous arcs of red and orange, lighting the valley like many small, falling suns.

H. Alder

UNREST
after Max Richter's Sleep

The woman is drifting somewhere
between day and night, light and dark.

Dark robed, she slips from the radio,
head covered, leads a camel across a desert,

joins other slow camels, tall as ships sailing.
A swell of orange flamed bodies sway to and fro.

She lifts the horizon to her eyes, reads a message
of long shadows, watches a voice that climbs alone.

She can hear no feet, just a rattle:
a rain-stick of rhetoric ready to tip up a storm.

The woman shakes her head, ear rocks roll. There is no rain.
Just the unrelenting fall of politician's speeches.

The sea fills, spills into a red starred sky, lungs balloon with brine.
A mist rolls in. No-one can see beyond the next rusting hull.

She tips her head sideways, sand trickles from her ear: brain sand.
Grains dislodge; they've been building up for years. The truth falls out.

A mouth full of sea biscuits and she's gasping, swallowing a shift of land.
There's a wail sidewinding across a tessellated terrain. Bodies shimmer.

A fish disappears like a snake's tail. Then there's a gap, a silence.
A chasm opens. Wide-eyed she looks into a black sky;

a small creature is curled beneath a bear's paw
and Zeus's eyes follow her like bullets.

Marion Oxley

SWIMMING
POOL

You hear the murmur when you wake up.
The buses are murmuring,
and the early taxis to Heathrow.
The trees moan with exhaustion.

The bed covers cough when you slide out.
Your feet on the wood have a parched throat
and your bag rasps when you pack it.
The door is needy and sighs.

Outside, you try to shush the cold air
but it asks breathy questions and
your feet ask sharper ones
why what why what why what.

In the changing room the air con
is keeping up a desperate stream of conversation
now and you pull your cap over your ears
too tightly. Shut up.

Your thighs say sensible things like
hush and don't listen and they
tut you as you walk to the edge.

The water wheezes as you enter it
too violently, and your skin shrieks
and then

quiet.

Your body and the water are all that is.
You move to the water's jellied breaths.
You are secretive as a turbot under ice.
The tiles, the splash, the way your shoulders
roll like dunes and your legs are kelp.

When your Atlas arms haul you back into
the garrulous world, you feel lumbering.
The shower keeps up its stream of vitriol,
the hair dryer complains and your back
cracks an explctive.

The trains are fretting today.

Kathryn Haworth

TODAY

Scrambled eggs,
black coffee,
a heavy sigh
at the morning yawning ahead.
Shake off the dusk from a night of dreams:
put on the mask
and grab today by the throat.

Deborah Maudlin

TIME TRAVELLER

One has to be ready for anything
on a day like this. When you step
into the lift to join the others
who pretend you don't exist
(or perhaps they just can't see you)
and the door concertinas with a clatter
and the smell of stale tobacco
combined with the antique design
conspires to take you back
to a time fifty years ago,
it can't help but strike you how
it all seems like no time at all
and that all those early mornings
sitting on the bus in the rain
warm in your overcoat were for nothing.
Now, at least, we're going up in the world
to the third floor: the cage
rocks a little, then stops.
What am I letting myself in for?
you wonder but whatever passes
through your mind, so what?
You'll find out soon enough.

Dominic Rivron

NEIGHBOURS   The man next door
                is moving stuff about.
                I can hear
                the high-note scrape
                across the floor
                as he pulls the chairs
                and the dull knocking
                as if he's lugging heavy boxes
                up and down the stairs,
                dumping them among
                the clutter I saw in there once
                and which I guess must be
                still there although
                you never know.
                Sometimes I see him
                from the upstairs window
                out in the garden
                smoking cigarettes
                or trying to get a signal
                on his mobile phone
                or sitting on a plastic chair
                doing nothing.
                Sometimes he looks up
                at my tree and once
                he turned and just for a moment
                our eyes met although
                I think we both pretended
                otherwise.
                So much of what we see
                (he and I)'s
                the same but different, seen
                from a slightly different angle
                as it is. Sometimes perhaps
                he hears me playing the guitar
                but if he does he never says
                and I, for my part,
                still have no idea
                exactly what
                he keeps in all the boxes.

                Dominic Rivron

WIDOWER

Eyes hot, back cold,
slumped over grass-rake,
the lucid striker
of a casual match,
poses a question.

Master of the thermosphere,
he sets the chaos-dragon loose
beyond his pergola.
His flames vault themselves,
slap the air.
Destruction lisps
in sap-boiling stalks.

Commander of white oceans
ebbing across the afternoon,
he has an argument with heaven,
a mighty plume that makes for the sky,
arches in the breeze
and slumps on the wreckage of summer,
hollyhocks slanting to a yellowing year,

and seeps into kitchens
so neighbours' trays of china clink
as they sniff the air,
sense a breath of invasion,
eye each other and ask
Has someone got a fire?

Martin Reed

Annual Visit

A night jug of piss by our bed
in my brother-in-law's attic.
Chilly, almost damp –
something to bear.

Out from under the duvet
that crackles in its black cover,
I make a start on fetching us tea,
squeeze sideways past the stairlift.

Stranded outside her room
one floor down, my teenage niece,
forty next year, calls out *Mum!* –
as though she has forgotten

I am her aunt, forgotten
that her mother is confined
to a dining room
we never go in for meals.

Dad told me to let him be,
my niece achieves.

From the hospital bed
on permanent loan,
her mother is crying out his name
through two closed doors

and the all-night murmur
of the World Service.

I edge my way back up
to our bed, a mug in each fist,
the biggest I can find
to make the drinking last.

Jenny Hockey

BUS PASS

A passport to purgatory
with no request stops
and one final destination.

Blank eyed, killer cold,
I look just like some shifty cove
of interest to the police –
a drug baron or someone who
does dreadful things to cats.

I place my effigy face down,
wait for the electronic ping
which says I am still me,
then find a seat.

The bus, packed full
as a milkman's crate
with silver tops,
is loud with chat.

– These car wash people are all Russian.
– They'll soon get finished then.
– Isn't it funny – you often find
something you haven't lost.

Museum Street. The conversation's stilled.
We shuffle off, take up our own affairs
– optician, dentist, hospital for tests –
all necessary measures for survival.
That way we can eke out a few more years.
But still
the journey matters more than the arrival.

Ian Stuart

HOME
COMFORTS

bleak faced
weather
worriers
wake
and weather man
is warning

kettle on
before mind clicks
with sweet rewards
for nothing

slide into passivity
in misty morning moments
the screen reflects an ageing face
but we'll think quickly for you

let's talk about
rain water
traffic dilemmas
we only know sensations

ladies and gents
it's outrage a.m.
to your procrastination
stations

let's wash our brains
with puppet dance
nauseating obedience

calm
storms
of thought
with tangled tales
a hundred hours stolen

morning mirror
modern fire
mouths slow subconscious whispers

time tick tocks
and the screen is on
are you a consumer or a creator?

Steve Beadle

SALES ASSISTANTS

One has straightened her hair,
streaked blonde into the brown,
is ready for home.

One has a spaniel's mop,
wears double opaques, she says –
on thin, world-weary legs.

Want some help? they call out,
already unhooking summer stock,
emptying sale rails into my arms.

I tumble into a cubicle, cowering
before the mirror – my beige body,
in ill-matched pants and bra,

hear them form a committee
with Dee, my double-denim friend.
Calvin Klein is so totally you!

they shout — and soon no item
of work or sleep or leisurewear
escapes their designs

on a dream of my life to come
in halter-neck top and sequinned mini –
a shoo-in for nights in Dubai.

Back in my winter layers
I shoulder improbable bargains
out into January's dog end of dusk.

They fold away the week.

Jenny Hockey

YOU AND THAT PIANO

Monday

You get off the train at Brighton station. Your office building is right next door. It wouldn't make sense for you to drive. You don't own a car, anyway, and you'd like to keep it that way. Besides, you've taken this journey for over two decades. It's the only thing you know.

You put your ticket in the machine. You've been meaning to get one of those travel cards, but you're used to doing it this way. You don't like change. It scares you. A lot of things scare you.

You go through the barrier. That's where you see an old wooden piano with a plastic sign attached to it that reads: PLAY ME. You've never seen it before. When did it get here? you think. More importantly, how did it get here?

You stare at that sign for a while, completely transfixed. It's just you and that piano – nothing else matters to you in that moment. Then you check your watch – you're late for work.

Tuesday

You arrive at the station to find a crowd of people gathered around the piano. You see a man sitting on the piano bench. He's tall with broad shoulders, and he wears what you can only assume is his trademark fedora hat. But you don't care what he looks like – all you care about is the way he plays that piano. His hands seem to dance effortlessly along the ivory keys as he plays "Nuvole Bianche" by Ludovico Einaudi – one of your favourite pieces.

You stand there and watch the man, biting your fingernails. Your mother always told you not to bite your nails – that it was a dirty habit – but you can't help yourself.

You've *never* been able to help yourself.

You start to think that you couldn't possibly be as good as the man in the fedora hat. You think that he must be a professional – if he plays like that, then surely he *must* be a professional. But when he finishes his piece, the man returns to the nearby coffee stand, puts on his apron and goes back to work.

Then it's just you and that piano again.

Dream Catcher 41   96

Wednesday

You convince yourself that today is the day: today is the day that you're finally going to do it. You just had a feeling when you woke up this morning – that's when you decided you were going to do it. In fact, you think that this decision was made by someone else – a higher power, perhaps.

But despite all of the build-up, you chicken out at the last second, like the coward you are.

Thursday

You've called in sick today. But you're not sick. You're not the kind of person who does this sort of thing. In fact, it's the first time you've called in sick in over fifteen years. But you've still come to the station. You felt like you *had* to come – you felt like you *needed* to come. You don't care if anyone from work sees you. That's the least of your concerns.

You run your right hand along the piano, your wrinkled fingertips gently touching the ivory keys. You do this carefully enough that you don't make a sound – it's very important to you that you don't make a sound.

Friday

You know you've said it before, but you're convinced that today is *definitely* the day that you are going to play.

When you get to the station, you put your ticket in the machine. Then the barrier opens. You march straight over to that piano, like a woman on a mission. But before you can get there, two small children beat you to it.

They sit at the piano bench and slam their tiny hands down on the keys, creating what can only be described as an unpleasant racket. Where are their parents? you think. And why are they letting their children misbehave like this? That's why you've never had any children of your own. You just don't get them. They don't get you, either. And now, because of *them*, you've missed your chance.

Saturday

You're not working today. You don't work on weekends. It's one of the only things you like about your job. But you're still drawn to that piano – it seems to have great power over you, over your life. It sits there, in the middle of the station, taunting you. Mocking you. You can hear it whisper in your ear. You can't make out what it's saying, but you know *why* it's saying it.

You can't take much more of it. You feel like screaming at the top of your lungs. But that's what it *wants* you to do. So instead, you sit down in the middle of the station, and you weep.

<u>Sunday</u>

The station is quiet today. You think that you might be ready to do it. You've been thinking about it for a while now. You've just been sitting there on a bench at the station, thinking.

You get up out of your seat, and you walk. You're drenched in sweat, but you just don't care anymore. You approach the piano. It looks at you. You take one final breath. Then you sit down at that piano, and you play.

Thomas Morgan

A flock of pigeons spends its days
sitting on the roof of the hotel.
Most of the time I can't see them
from where I sit but I know they're
almost certainly there,
sitting and thinking about
whatever it is pigeons think about,
because every now and then
they take flight *en masse*,
swooping down the alley,
round the square and back
and when they do
they fill my window
just for a moment
as with precision
they reach their apogee,
pulling out of a steep dive
towards the cobblestones
and heading up again
to disappear from view.

Dominic Rivron

RAT JUNCTION

Our fenced-in ground,
borrowed for whatever time we have,
is laced and tunneled by a parallel network
of well-worn grooves and passages.

A track cuts through the chicken pen,
wanders by food-bins
around the greenhouse to an overhead line
along the fence-top that buffers
at next door's wild-bird feeder.

We eye each other from opposed platforms,
separate branches on the tree of life.
The portly fellow in dun overcoat
laments a missed connection,
sidles off to his underground rest-room.

Rats share whatever's brought to the nest,
nurse their injured,
communal and intelligent
eat human poison, die in drains,

are always re-born as wiser denizens
toting a nutty slink of fur,
better equipped for the long haul,
their tenantry bound to outlast ours.

Martin Reed

That was the spring you could walk down the middle of the road, stone cold sober, at 2 p.m., and no-one batted an eyelid. After a week of awkward elbow-bumps we settled for eyeing each other suspiciously above over-worked smiles. We texted exes with offers of support, and the moral high ground made molehills out of mountains. And you remembered that moles are blamed for tunnelling listeria under pasture-land, and that badgers are blamed for bovine TB, and rats vilified for the Black Death when it was in fact the parasites that caused it, the fleas that swelled with pride at their power. And you recalled John Donne's poem about the flea, the only metaphysical poet to make insect bites sexy as fuck. And that was the spring the leader of the free world called this the Chinese virus and said that he was looking forward to churches full of worshippers next Sunday, and the spring when some of us believed his delusional arrogance was the biggest contagious risk imaginable. And the spring when you mused that social distancing might result in a new chastity, and at the same time how lockdown would bring a spike in the birth-rate come Christmas. And the sky was so blue and the sun so warm it was hard to believe there would be a Good Friday before the Resurrection and, coming back to the rats for a minute, you caught the latest news bulletin and heard that Parliament was closing now, until after the Easter Recess. And each day you woke and heard birdsong in place of rush hour traffic you opened your lungs to the world and the air was like champagne.

Note.- This poem has been set to music by Matthew Ogleby.

Hannah Stone

ON THE
EDGE

Suburbia teetered on the edge.
Always unstable, it rocked and tilted,
swivelled to the sixties pulsing beat.

Seduced by the soft pad padding
of Hush Puppies on pebbled lino,
the locked-in promise of Tupperware,

Lazy Susan's sealed lips turned aside
to part on glacéd days of diazepam,
Babycham and Cherry B.

These were the turning away years
of Formica, white onyx fitted wardrobes.
The slow slide and quiet closing

of sex and matching twin beds,
static Bri-Nylon sheets, a pillow's crackle.
Lady Chatterley's Lover, carefully hidden

at the back of the musty, walnut bureau,
kept sly company with a tired
but well-read Reader's Digest.

Harsh pebble-dashed walls tore strips off
elbows, knees, a bleed of whispers
oozed through ill-fitting French windows.

The pink and grey flagged patio you'd laid
produced hairline cracks. The uneven garden
path stumbled on towards a newly built

creosoted shed. In dark, breathless space
words were tensely pruned,
a neat topiary of resignation.

Pale, liver-spotted hands damp as frog skin
whet shears that blink in strokes of sunlight.
Precision feels good balanced on soiled palms.

The tight-lipped hedge gasps
at the steely snap of finality.

Marion Oxley

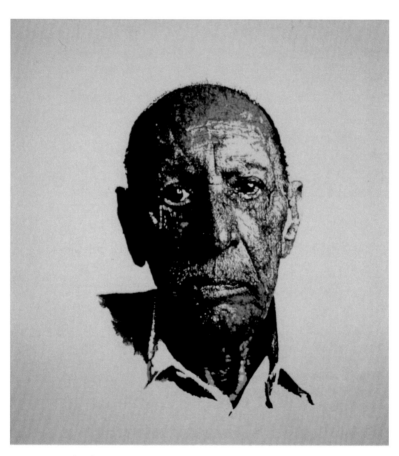

Igor Stravinsky

A BRIEF HISTORY OF SPROTBROUGH HALL

1

With the dogs in Bewicke-Copley's plantation, I notice three layers
of green dressed stone buried by a churchyard's weight of ivy.

Lift the clamp of leaves and woody vines, unearth a gateway
between two pillars, mason-trimmed, hinge-work rusting on old pivots.

Ninety years ago, the big house was dropped through its own cellars;
before that, where the dogs snuffle and point, lay acknowledged order.

Pruned shrubs, gravelled footpaths. Three gardeners and their ragged boys
dragged from the village daily to tidy the Baronet's landscape.

The wall was taller then, no ivy dragging it over the river's cliff,
footpaths by the Don, fountains and a pool, things just as they should be.

Returned to wilderness, uncertain tracks wander through knots of nettles,
thistles, birch stands, an unruly copse: Edwardian clarities overgrown.

2

Beside the motorway, this morning jammed tight going north, hardly easier
south, the path curves towards open ground, ascends a short slope.

Threadbare tree-clumps dwindle to nothing, a thin footbridge spans the A1,
not wide enough for two handfuls of dogs to pass without growls and hackles.

The old estate ripped open in the Fifties by diesel powered shovels on half-tracks,
men in dungarees wearing rubber boots and flat caps, flinging picks,

drills and spades into the land's core. A wedge of it shifted, dug out and dumped,
but the river crossed, the town bypassed. Upstream are railway bridges, one

Beeching-hit and broken, left to decay and thickly tagged, Daz from Edlo
with his mates banished into another tense. Rolling like old wagons

down the Don's inclines and terraced woods, the years rattle watch chains,
monied vowels, the big house, redflushed faces toasting the Empire.

Their voices quit this scrap of Yorkshire but didn't vanish. Like the pipistrelles
dodging in loops down the gorge, they simply moved on, found new roosts.

David Harmer

GARDEN

Granting us space, I leave the veranda,
where you preside like a marble queen.
I fix my eye on the butterfly zone
at the far end of the garden.

We are enclosed and, it seems, quite alone,
perhaps no other visitors today.
I caress a wall with its weeping grapes.
It radiates the built-up heat.

A trickling waterfall soothes senses,
alleviates echoes of your complaints.
I loiter by the disjointed sundial,
then skirt the maze I know so well

to the central pond of disagreement,
forsaken but for a tin flamingo,
a brace of nymphs coated with egg-white,
to encourage lichen and moss,

the way you like things – distressed and semi-wild,
in this fey, fantastical romance you make.
I favour koi carp and you want frogs
 – and tadpoles are a fishfeast, yes.

Avoiding the thicket of untame thorn,
I withdraw to my palace of flowers,
which you raid, I know, with sharp secateurs,
coveting my amaryllis,

to be draped on the statues of Flora,
of Titania and Proserpina.
On those stone effigies, offered wreaths wilt,
while you sing in your fluted dress.

I will command scraped, then, a new mini-lake for you
and lay an antique tulip in your lap.
The black or the blue is my privilege to choose
 – because I am the gardener.

Clive Donovan

The bread aisle was stripped long before Maundy Thursday; the Queen had to mail her widow's mite to grateful subjects and feet remained unwashed. Wine boxes flew off the shelves. The moon was unusually vigilant after still, cloudless days, and the birdsong almost deafened the angels who hovered in the wedding-white blossom of damson, plum, pear trees. The silence on Good Friday was an echo of itself before 24/7 shopping, a day when the Christian world held its breath, and hot-cross buns made a single, eagerly anticipated appearance, spices embalming dried fruit, dough springy to the touch. Noli me tangere was the phrase on everyone's lips. Stones were raked away from mass graves on Hart Island, where prisoners in Hazmat suits shift body-bags collected from apartment blocks by forklift trucks. Lazarus waited his turn in vain. The Gardener wept.

Hannah Stone

SO YOU'RE RIGHT (GOD DOESN'T CARE)

Already the woods are shrinking
into evening. Leaves
have hit the ground hard
and lie like shattered biscuit.
Light unhooks itself from trees.

I've come to pray, and update
my resentments instead.
Not the gasp of a tree,
not the bone-hollow thrum
of a pigeon, can stop me now.

I must be a saint, from my diary
(I'd welcome a footnote on that:
your exemplary rudeness,
new records I set
for not taking offence).

I've left makeshift arrows
but still I get lost in a silence
that looks like the words
Again. Keep very still.
Now let's try this again.

Carolyn Oulton

It's always bitter sweet.
I slip into the northern twang,
taste again the salt tang of its vowels,
the kick of consonants hard as granite.
Echoes rise from cobbled streets
where yacking tongues still blather,
seeking to set the world to rights
between the back-to-backs.

The moors are massaged by light.
An easterly wind sweeps across
gorse and heather, flattening
the face of the grass. I watch it comb
the fleeces of curly-horned sheep
that have grazed on the hillside
for generations and now huddle together
in the shadow of a dry-stone wall.

Midges gather at dusk.
They swarm round street-lamps,
rising in spirals like the smoke
that swirled around my youth.
I catch a sudden whiff of Woodbines,
steaming coffee in the Wimpy,
the dank scent of mushrooms
picked in early autumn mist.

Dawn restores the long-forgotten
sound of distant hooves on stone.
I hear the slow clip-clop of time
beneath my window and see again
that old familiar childhood horse
that plods across the centuries,
the rags and bones of memories
crammed on his ramshackle cart.

Doreen Hinchliffe

OWL'S EYES

From Foxes Row, past the hen runs,
mushrooms fresh as frost melting
into grass; down valley sides, fast

as feet crumbling soil; twin tunnels
our concrete playground, the broken lip:
its pool and forestry firs strangling

in tall brush. We jumped over, splashed,
looked for tiddlers. We bounced logs across
water, dared them to break, found balance.

Owl's Eyes, child size, the plosh
of feet dancing side to side, head
bent forward, racing each other

under tons of earth left for ghost
trains on a Beeching line, scare and dare
into the haze of darkness, damp walls

reflecting light, opening an eclipse
into the woods. I stood with leaves watching
a deer licking dew from ripples. The startle,

antlers crowning air and gone. That space:
a folk tale, and I was there,
a suckered arrow in my hand, a hoof print.

Mike Alderson

GRIMSTON

North Grimston sits where the valleys join,
its church raised where roads and paths converge,
that bear the faithful, that bear the dead,
that bear the infants to be blessed in its stone font.
And who knows which Saxon, Viking, carved on this hard bowl
the Last Supper, and Christ crucified.

The landscape's dense with barrows, tumuli,
and bones of the past – Bronze and Iron Age, Roman –
lost villages, their ancient worship sites
still marked by churches, chapels,
and the hills rich with sheepwalks, cattle, arable.

From Grimston Brow the chalk-specked fields of the top
give way to pasture; and beyond the Wold's edge lies
the old lost lake bed, moors to the North,
the broad Vale to the West and beyond that,
north and south like a distant wall,
the grit and limestone spine of a harder, bleaker land,
unblest 'til long after the Word trod these soft, green hills.

John Gilham

THE MARCH HARE

The March Hare follows his ancient track,
tasting the air for signs of Spring,
running,
jumping,
his feet trying to reawaken the earth
from such a long sleep.

Deborah Maudlin

i don't remember   only
falling from cloud and heavier then
          like stone to earth   a plummeting
                    a drunken interruption   cheeky sod
          to land like laughter on a sleepy afternoon
     and my body jolted   fit to shatter carapace
          a shock that shook alive
                    and woken senses into newness
                              felt a foreign light irradiate my angularity
and people watched, yes, wanting show
          so not to disappoint   – i don't remember but i do –
               i crawled
                    like
                         this
and though the voice said   deviate   procrastinate   i didn't
               so with all of them looking
                         gathered up the fragments of my dignity
                              i crossed the line and over the edge
                         i did it
               i just flew

Richard Kitchen

A CALLOUS SCHEME

Spring is a callous scheme
as it will arrive whether
I'm alive or not,
its beauty cruel, relentless.

Old Woman Creek will continue,
implacably, to rage at its banks,
abating on its own terms
in the lulling of summer.

The lilac will relinquish
its sweet redolence mercilessly
outside our bedroom window.
Intoxication is the plot.

The trillium will dance,
those delicate liars,
in the woods upon the loam,
in supposedly perfect trinities.

The rude apple blossoms
will burst open, all remorseless
bastards, a blizzard in May,
drifts of petals everywhere.

The pitiless grasses will rise,
too tender, too blithe
on my fingertips,
so damn green it is heartache.

The doe's fawns will stumble
into the meadow, the darling
little idiots playing on sentiment,
a deliberate torture.

The lake will mirror the sky,
blue their romance, an ineludible
infatuation, a tryst with
no regard for me. No mercy.

David Sapp

TOUCHING WILD (3-8-83)

What instinct drives vocation,

feral, to pursue your task,

perform it savagely,

invest it with your life?

This is all, no choice, no deviation,

what you need and are designed to do:

to navigate your way,

to stalk the truth,

to capture, study, understand

and let it fly again.

The boy who talks to birds

recognises something in the trees,

a life, a soul in tandem, waits

to feel its untamed breath.

So crouch your monkey squat,

so stretch your longing arms:

innocence

returning to your eyes, peace

seeping into blood, a smile

of wonder bright in bone,

a *yes* that flows from land to brain

and sends you

glowing

as you

go,

the boy with dancing hands.

What poetry informs this muscle,

      sinew's syntax in articulation

         as you walk

            and as you stroke a living being

            from the page,

            to coax it out of hiding?

          Lure it to reveal itself

         as you and it emerge from essence:

       image gathered in the eye

     and in the holding meaning.

Lines connecting wood with fingers, earth with mind,

  forge sentences with which to shout your joy

     WHAT SPIRIT ANIMATES THIS PLACE?
     MY CREATURES KNOW

         WHAT LOVE IS IT I FEEL?
         MY LANDSCAPE TEACHES

            ALL THEIR NATURE ONE IN UNIVERSE
            ALL INSTRUMENTS IN TUNE

           AND SINGING
         I AM FREE
        TO KNOW MYSELF
      TO BE
     AS I COME HOME

Richard Kitchen

The Hungry One

Part tongue
part intestine
my tar-black back
is surgical
glue sealing
the long
incision in
the earth's skin
the suture
that was made
when they
implanted
me inside
her. In a way
I am the only
thing holding
her together
my bride
of Frankenstein
or at least I
like to think
so. Although
I imagine
after my makers
have been gone
a few million
years
her skin
will heal
and disgorge me
like pus from
a whitehead
or seal over
me and I will
become
another
of her scars.

I am one
of the wires
of the net
they have made
to snare her.
Metal furballs
cough along
my gullet
with a smell
of burning rubber
and all along
me are
slowly
digested
the remains
of animals
I have skinned
and flattened.
See this badger
I have made
into a shapeless
rubber sack.
This squirrel's
pelt I have torn
from its armature
of tendons and
bones. This pile
of feathers
which adheres
to me was
once a bird.
In time they will
all sink so far
into my skin
they will become
indistinguishable
from me. I am

my own belly
and am forever
emptily
growling
at the cows
who stare
at me from
the safety
of their pasture
behind the
barbed-wire
fence. Little
do they know how
I am helping
to devour
their young
by conveying
them along
my rolling
tongue
to the places where
they slaughter
them. I am
Leviathan's
distended
gut. But I will
not be able
much longer
to feed him
once he runs
out of his raw
materials
starves and abandons
me. I do not know
why they made
me always to be
so hungry.

Taliesin Gore

THE ROAD TO MONIAIVE

Follow the bizzin Nith
to begin with – that merge
of mythland and earth, turning
into the curve of home hills.

Who asked to be born
into a warrior family?
Which woman ever wished
for her name to be sung

by soldiers in their hundreds
and thousands, hungry for
hearthstones and female company?
No woman I know could volunteer

to pay that price for fame; a waste
of courage to become cannon fodder.
The road narrows to one way –
and a plain brown town of local stone.

What a year for caorainn –
seeding with rich berries,
redder than blood-stained memory
on the borders of late summer.

At the Craigdarroch Arms renovations
erased the rough portrait of Annie Laurie
behind red flock wallpaper and a thirty-inch
TV screen. Dream on, romantics –

That's history for you –
gone when you come back to find
what you thought you saw before,
the fireplace bright as a living heart.

Briar Wood

A REFLECTION

I believe that the river runs in me
and this is something special, something
to compensate for the many mistakes.

I believe that the world tilts and ripples
and the art of staying on your feet
is to obey the rhythm of the current.

I believe that my head is a pool
of small fish, mud brown and inedible,
the sort you weigh quickly and throw back.

I believe that the moorhen's complaint
and the muffled boom of a distant weir
are the sounds of home.

I believe that when winter gives way to summer,
the grass will rise above the meadow mud
and dock leaves draw the nettles' sting.

I believe that in spring
when ducklings form a line behind their mother
there is always one who veers towards the other bank.

Sometimes I believed I was going to drown.

David Lukens

My civilisation has been trampled underfoot. Chaos set loose in every nook and cranny.

On Christmas Eve my wife and baby fell seriously ill. The illness had gathered momentum throughout the previous weeks and we were at a loss as to how to proceed. Luckily, Sophie's father is a retired anaesthetist and, on seeing the condition of my family, he acted decisively. Not for him, the wait for a GP's appointment. Albie was rushed to Sick Kids and Sophie headed straight to the Royal Infirmary. His actions proved timely. Being a parent is a crazy golf course where the pins are moved the very moment you strike the ball.

Suffice it to say I spent Christmas Day at the bed of my child in the High Dependency Unit, his little body fully spent. A huge pink blancmange of an infection had taken hold of his left eye. His arm was entrapped in a complex scaffolding of metal tubes and valves through which antibiotics flooded his little system. Painkillers were syringed into his mouth to a strict timetable. His fair hair hung limply over his brow. Three miles distant lay my wife. My world was collapsed to two hospital beds. Not only was she wan and weak but she had lost her voice so it was difficult to comfort her. I would hold her hand and look into her eyes and think about how I might feed the cat.

That was the start of my vigil. Nothing sorts a man out better than a spell out of his comfort zone. I sat clamped to the plastic of a bedside chair, stupid anxieties filtering through my mind. I was expecting a Times wine delivery and could see the box lying empty outside my door. The car was due in for a service. My thoughts were disturbed by rumblings from a lady opposite. I had spotted her tiny baby in a far too big bed, a child wearing a pink all-in-one with matching woolly hat and mitts whose life was recorded in a machine beside the bed. How tiny must the bones be inside the shell of that baby. How would you count the miniature vertebrae running along the baby's back?

I opened my eyes. The child's mother was on her knees. She was praying, emptying her wishes before God. What did she seriously expect to happen? Would the roof open and a large kindly finger lower itself on to the baby's beating heart and wipe away the misery?

I felt an anger rise up inside me. She had long, fair hair which fell over her face. The tops of her pants were exposed where she bent over. I wanted to tap her on the shoulder and say, medicine not mutterings will win the day. I wanted to describe the footballers who, on entering the field of play, cross themselves. What is the God fella supposed to do? He is bound to upset someone. Logically speaking, two teams can't win. The laws of the game, like the laws of nature, are master of all they survey.

I watched the woman stagger to her feet, her legs frozen. She held the bedstead to steady herself. She smiled across at me and, unable to stop myself, I wagged a finger and mouthed "no" and shook my head for emphasis. She sat herself down, turning her chair away from me. I wasn't crushed by her actions. She had her drivel to hang on to, fingertips tightly hoping for the best, while I had the verdict of science upon which to stand. We would see which outcome prevailed.

The lights were dimmed but manners had gone to the wall. Movies blasted out from phones and computer pads as though each bed was its own planet circling in outer space. I realised we were all lost in our own selfishness. Common courtesy had become a thing of the past.

Sleep was impossible. A kindly nurse passed me a thin mattress and I imagined the imprints of the ghosts of previous parents who had tossed and turned on its sagging surface. Little Albie slept fitfully.

"Speak to me," I whispered. "Give me one of your temper tantrums, please. I will never be angry with you again."

He didn't belong on that huge sea of a bed. His very skin rebelled against the strange smells and hard bars of the bed. Throughout the night, nurses appeared to further flood his body. In the morning he refused cereal and settled for the comfort of yoghurt. Daylight was a relief of sorts and when my dad appeared I set off to visit Sophie. The smells of the ward clung to my clothes and in leaving the ward I felt I was leaving nothing behind.

The days after Christmas proved to be the turning point. Albie's eye slowly came back into view. The doctors were pleased with his progress and Dr Hubbard whom I hit it off with, he being a fellow Ayrshire man and Kilmarnock supporter, spoke to me about how close to death Albie had been. The fear had been that sepsis would seep into Albie's organs which would inevitably call it a day. We shared a joke about the foolish woman living in a land of superstition.

Five years have passed since I left that Christmas behind. Albie started primary school four months ago. He could read before he first passed through the school doors and he loves to kick a ball, running, running, across open spaces with a determination that has served him well throughout his first five years.

I still smell the hospital in my nostrils and I catch myself looking at Albie expecting to see a pink slab of disease attached to his face but more than that, fresh as it had taken place only hours ago, is the conversation which took place with the little lady who was filled to bursting with prayers.

She approached me as I gathered up my bags. Sophie was outside with Albie, renewing bonds and breathing in fresh air blowing across the Southern Uplands.

I feared what she might say, afraid that she was aware of my conversations with Dr. Hubbard.

I got my bit in first.

"How is the little mite?"

We stood in two different worlds, I at the top of the mountain, she bogged down in the foothills.

"Your son has come through it all," she said.

Her jealousy was understandable. I had not seen her baby out of the cot. I had never heard him cry. I could only think his continued silence a bad sign.

"How is your baby?"

"He might die," she said.

"That can't be right," I said.

"Thousands of babies die every day. He is no more special than them."

In her eyes there was a defiance against the weight of the material world. She was standing on tiptoe as if in closeness she might better get her message across.

"I have been studying you all week," she continued. "You never let go, always determined to see it through. Remember you have been given a gift. Don't forget about the giver of the gift."

I didn't know what to say.

"You are a brave dad. I had to tell you this before you go. We will never meet again."

How could she be so sure? I had things I wanted to clear up. Where was her self-pity? She didn't fit into my picture of the world. My civilisation was built upon pounds and pence and the hard facts of life. She had me worried.

I think about her regularly. I couldn't disentangle her notion of a magical giver from the perfect chain of facts which had saved Albie's life. I have never lost sight of her small, radiant face with the long fair hair and sweet red lips. Recently, I came across a slow moving lady pushing a pram across the expanse of the Meadows. I was at a distance so I couldn't be sure if it was her. I made to catch her up but I faltered. I imagined a baby in her pram, a baby with quiet limbs and a silent face.

She was wrong about me. I have little courage and few serious thoughts. I was a product of a civilisation which fed me and kept my family warm but she has changed me. I no longer believe in the constancy of events. Tomorrow is a foreign country. I take nothing for granted, not the walk to the supermarket, not the delivery of the mail. I have taken to leaving the house earlier and earlier. One day I will meet myself coming back. I expect a traffic jam at any moment. I cannot look at the blood-red sun of a morning without thinking of my son's eye and when I close the door and pull the curtains tight at the end of another day I expect the bones of dead children to crawl beneath my windowsills.

Stewart J. Lowe

YOUR FEAR

What he had, the guy
with no cheek, his back teeth,
cheekbone, on view,
I don't know, but I tried
to stop you seeing him
as you waited your turn
for chemo to fight
cancer in your jaw.

Your fear, worse than death,
was that your face would
be eaten away, that none
of us would look at you
without a wince, all force
ourselves to sit with you.

Back home, you asked about
his missing cheek, the bone,
and, did I see, the staff
couldn't look at him.

I'd like to call your fear
misplaced. Like to say
I'd have been strong for you
(the cliché confirms your fear),
but I never had to force
my face to face your face.

Because you died soon after,
your face, at least, intact,
though lined and shrunk
by pain. Something
of the gazelle still,
as your breath stopped
and the lion dragged you off.

Malcolm Povey

GROUNDED

You wake suddenly, having dreamt for months
of turning restlessly in your seat
on a trans-Atlantic flight, one hot cheek
against a cushion, the other air-conditioned, cold.

Outside the waves are always pretty, and twice a day
the plane's shadow dances on their surface. The nurses
bring trolleys of food steaming beneath foil lids
and hand out plastic cutlery. One of the passengers

tries to cut his wrist. The doctors announce
they are clear to land but there may be some turbulence.
Please fasten your seatbelts and stow luggage
under the seat in front.

When you awake a guitar lies broken on the floor.
Only the strings hold it together.
A stewardess marks your chart on the wall.
Today is Tuesday.

Your family look worried, their voices out of tune,
and your daughter speaks more than she used to.
Soon she will be teaching you how to talk.
The pilot says in these winds it may be some time.

Robin Vaughan-Williams

Another time, I won't bring Philip,
he's so distracting, talking of
where he got the train, that Saturday
and of a shop he didn't like
the best pub for jazz
and how he misses the river,
its slow presence.

On and on, as if this place
is all about him – the hospital,
there for his convenience, to die in,
the view from his flat, the best view,
the cemetery monuments' purpose
to witness his wanderings.

I won't bring him.
There's more to here than words,
for all through his time this city's tide was out,
after the fishing, before the Larkin Trail.

John Gilham

My heart skips a beat when he calls me at the end of his nightshift. Tells me he's been proning patients. Takes 7 ICU staff to wrap them in a sheet (like a Cornish pasty, he says), holding up the mesh of lines that snake like veins escaped from arms and neck. (Think art installation, minus formaldehyde, for now.) Once prone, the patient's head should be turned every two hours, to prevent pressure sores. He admits to concern about PTSD. Imagine coming round, drugged sight striving to process the blank stare of the corpse on the other bed in the bay. In full PPE he is forbidden to comfort a nurse with tears streaming down her face. At the end of his shift, he was served coffee by furloughed pilots, super keen to greet him in the hospital's new First Class Lounge, their sleeves swathed with braid. I send him trills of birdsong, blue skies full of blossom. I begin to wonder if I should say sorry to God, ask if he'll have me back.

Hannah Stone

RETURN TO BARMOUTH

There's a long bridge where
the trains slow on the single line –
and a footway, alongside.

Six hours by six hours
the clear cold water slips beneath
it calls – *Come.*

For I will always remember, here, in plain sight
the shifting sand, the suction,
the outgoing tide, the unheard cries for help:

an early, unwelcome,
confrontation with mortality
I, even now, have failed to exorcise.

John Gilham

The man in the yellow tie settles himself in the corner of the room. No one invited him, but he appears at ease – at home, even – as he clears his throat of wasps and other irritations. He begins to speak, trying out common languages until he clicks into something we all understand, before paring down complexities until he settles into the appropriate lexis. *We shouldn't feel alone*, he tells us, trying out tones and inflections until we believe him, or at least don't disbelieve him, which is good enough amidst the chaos of rolling news and birdsong. So as not to offend him, we pass surreptitious notes about the morality of turning him out or letting him stay, though long before we reach any conclusion he is part of the family. Maybe he's a lost uncle, or perhaps he married one of our sisters or daughters. The photos on the mantelpiece are inconclusive, but there he is, sure enough, the knot in his yellow tie waxing and waning like the Moon as it marks out the decades in men's fashion. On the television, someone is talking about either wood anemones or wooden enemies, the distinction being purely semantic in this time of isolation, and the important point is the reminder of connections to things beyond ourselves. The man in the yellow tie is older now – perhaps our grandfather – and he nods to himself on the edge of sleep. *We shouldn't feel alone*, he says.

Oz Hardwick

"I wake up lying on my back, unable to move. He's smiling down at me..."

"Who is, love?"

"And I... ask him, where I am. He just says I'm a dissident. Says I'm going to start a new life. Not going to be... like I am, anymore. Not, you know, the way I'm always curious, always asking questions..."

"I know. I know, love."

"And always thinking of how things could be better. He's got a syringe. He calls it 'the solution' – the stuff in it. It's on one of those steel trolleys like they have in hospital. Beside the table, whatever it is, that I'm lying on. He knows I can't see well so he holds it right near me, next to my face. I can feel my hands going cold..."

Her words trailed off.

He knew he'd reached that tough pass, just like in his old work: the witness too distressed to go on.

"It's over, love, you're safe, you're at home, with me."

He stole an arm under her.

"You can tell me everything. Can't you?"

"Mmm..." She smiled at him.

He made the tiniest of verbal noises, perfected over the years. The one that said, 'I'm on your side. I'm listening.'

"He's talking about the Project. It's their invention, he says, it's part of their latest Program. It's... for... dissidents. Like me. Like us. Tad... I try and move but there are straps. They're broad, soft, won't leave a mark. He's asking me if I knew about the previous Program. Of course I know! Those... so-called medical implants. Learned Responses. So... grossly overdone. The shocks: all the people who died, he's referring to them as 'collateral damage'! Our Party Leader!"

"Yes, I know."

"He's saying he regrets killing Jude because he could have brainwashed him instead! With the stuff in that bloody syringe! It almost made me glad they had killed him! 'Those whom the Gods would destroy' and all that. And he lets slip that the stuff's only just been developed, that's why they didn't... didn't..."

"Didn't use it on Jude?"

"Yes. Want to try it out on 'volunteer subjects' first. Referred to me, strapped to this bloody table, as a 'volunteer'! And a 'subject'! Because I was born in Britain: British subject. And he said, well I suppose it's true, I'm one of the best-known dissidents in our Neighborhood Defense Bloc.

"And when I say I don't want to volunteer, he pretends to get all sentimental. Says this stuff, this horrible stuff, is 'a gift, from the Project.' And that they'll get all upset if I turn it down. As if the Project has feelings.

Gift... it means Poison. In German. You know I learned French and German, at school. In Hampshire..."

"Yes, love. And some Polish. From me."

"And I have to keep quiet about it. Bloody Trump-junior and his foreign language ban."

They could each tell the other's thoughts. Their daughter, fluent in Polish, keeping it quiet: only had to keep it quiet for another month while she worked her notice as a meteorologist at Climate, Inc. Bricks through the windows, courtesy of the Denialists. With a bit of luck and a following wind she'd be out of territorial waters by October 22nd, and away: another Returner.

"So, British Subject," he smiled. "What happens next?"

"He's pulled up the bedside chair and sat down, sat next to me trying to be friendly. Just like you told me they did... at your work. The ones who use the Reid Technique. Step five: reassure. Look sincere. Oh God. He wants to tell me exactly what it's going to do to me. Do I really want to know? He starts,"

She mimicked his voice:

" 'First up, it don't destroy nothing. It ain't violent: ain't like one of those anti-psychotic drugs they gave to dissidents, the ones that got all the complaints, no sir. It works by overlayin'. Introducin' new behaviour patterns that you'll like: that you'll do. Been developed 'specially for people like you. How 'bout that?' "

"He says it works... like adverts do. You know the way they don't actually tell you anything about whatever it is they're advertising. The shampoo or whatever. They just use psychology to make you want to buy it. He says they - the teams of psychologists - know everything about what makes people want to do things. And the adverts they design... go... deep, in, without people being any the wiser. He called them 'enhanced' adverts. Well, commercials. Like people say here. And people buy, or believe, thinking they're choosing freely...

"But we're dissidents, the ones this method doesn't work on. Because we don't have a telly. Or those that do are kind of immune somehow. Immune to adverts. Enhanced adverts.

"He says, when the teams are absorbed in their work on designing these adverts, there's a chemical they produce in their brains. Like oxytocin when you trust, serotonin when you're happy, melatonin when you're sleepy. And they've let Program people come along and extract it.

"He shows me the syringe again: holds it up to press out all the air. Some of this awful stuff comes out. I'm... terrified. He talks about doing this several times, over years. Every six months bringing me back to this place, wherever it is, giving me more of this stuff and... obliterating my memory that I've been given it! And I think... I think..."

She looked away. He hoped he hadn't lost her. One of the first victims he'd ever interviewed, more than forty years ago now. In shock because, just a half-hour previously, a man had pulled a gun on her. She'd sat crying and, of all things, apologising. Because, she said, she was face-blind and wouldn't be able to recognize him again. "Not much use as a witness, am I?"

He'd had to start ever so gently: reassuring her the man was no longer around; waiting for her to stop crying. And he'd got her talking about how the man was standing, how he moved, how he held the gun. She'd been looking at his face. Sensible girl: you're less likely to get shot that way. But that meant she hadn't noticed the type of weapon: couldn't even tell a pistol from a revolver. Brits. Except: 'I noticed it was black with gold trimmings on'.

He got her to show how the man had held it: had he grabbed her? As a result, they'd worked out he'd been left-handed. And 'I was looking at his neck, because it had a cobweb drawn on it.' And 'No, sorry, I couldn't see the colour of his eyes: he had wrap-around shades on. They looked odd in his hair. It was pale and frizzy...'

"So, let me get this straight: we've got a pale frizzy-haired southpaw gunman with a cobweb tat on his neck and gold decals on his gun."

Pause.

"Now how many of them d'ya reckon we're going to have in this town, huh?"

And he'd got her to smile.

He had to use the same skills now, every time this happened. He wasn't going to ask her what she'd been thinking: no point, and too distressing.

"What does he do next?"

Present tense.

"I said if it were proper medical treatment, I'd have to... sign my consent. He said, I'd 'get consented' – can you believe a phrase like that - after I'd had the shot! I said that didn't count! I'd be a different person by then. But he said I'd still be me, just with 'enhanced behaviour'..."

She frowned, as if forcing herself to go on.

"He said I'd feel a lot happier. Being... the same as everybody else. Started talking about my school records going back decades, back to when our family first came to live here, in America. The new school had noticed what I was like and - my family never told me this – recommended me for some mental treatment! E.C.T.! My parents raised hell, and they were lucky: they managed to convince a doctor that electric shocks would risk killing me. My heart. I couldn't help smiling when he said they even went as far as to find a lawyer. When the school authorities found out about the lawyer, they backed down.

"He seemed to... genuinely believe that not buying stuff makes you unhappy. That curiosity makes you unhappy. That by doing this to me he'd be doing me a favour. And when I pointed out that we've next to no income he started talking about how nice our house is and we could raise money on it to buy stuff.

"I thought I'd floored him by telling him that going into debt would make me miserable."

"And that doesn't work? Doesn't convince him?"

"No. But it got him to tell me the real reason for what he was doing."

She frowned as she grappled with the idea.

"He says that without enough people buying things, the economy would collapse. There'd be massive unemployment and everybody would turn to crime. Whereas if we keep buying, the phrase he used was 'It'd keep the show on the road.' Doesn't sound very reassuring, does it?"

Tad shook his head.

"Then I thought of you! If I'm a 'dissident', what the heck are you? Off the scale! Fluent in a foreign language, repairing everything; one of the few people we know who's not plagued by some chronic illness needing daily doses of expensive medicines. Did they know? And if so, were they doing this to you as well?

"And if not, I'd... change, and I wouldn't know it was happening, and what would you think? You'd go off me, wouldn't you?

"Then I wondered if that's the reason so many people are getting divorced these days... and... it's good for 'them', the Project, because divorce causes people to... buy... more... stuff... oh Tad!

"I didn't want this. He stood up. He had that thing in his hand, in one hand. Still going on about wanting me to feel good: that I'd feel good. Didn't want the injection to hurt me, can you believe it after all that? Didn't want me to see it going in. So I made a point of keeping looking at my right arm, where he'd swabbed it earlier. He..."

He had to draw it all out: get her to tell it all.

Draw it out like poison.

Her gift.

As she'd smiled after her account of the hold-up all those years ago, he had handed her his card, saying she shouldn't hesitate to call if she remembered anything else, no matter how trivial.

And two days later at some ungodly hour she'd done exactly that. Called, and described a street corner she knew: he knew the one. Said she never wanted to set foot anywhere near it because he was there – the gunman. And then she had burst into tears and apologised, saying she shouldn't have bothered him because it was only a dream. She was nowhere nearby, she'd just dreamed it. And she'd hung up.

Bored in his squad car, he'd taken a turn round to that corner anyway. And who'd he noticed, standing right there, looking like he was up to no good at 3 a.m. in his wrap-around shades? Complete with his distinctive firearm, and a bag of coke for good measure: a nice easy arrest.

They'd let him question the man: a privilege for so young an officer. Listened in disbelief as all he'd done, after reciting him his Miranda Rights and reassuring him that 'we just wanna eliminate you from our enquiries' was ask the man for as thorough an account as he could give of the evening of the hold-up. Then realised what his game was as he went back and pressed, gently, on the weak points of the account. One by one, until the story unravelled. Unfashionable at the time, but effective...

"He forced my head away, with his other hand, and I felt the pressure on my shoulder..."

He felt the tension leave her: it was over. He held her, as he always did. Caroline. His witness. Safe.

Only one problem remained.

Unlike all the other predictive dreams she'd had: the shock second Trump presidency, the massive storm of '21 that would have ripped Mazzi and Fadida's roof off if they'd not, following her account of it at a party at their house, had repairs done first; the anti-immigrant riot in Seattle, of all places... unlike all those this dream, on being recounted, had a horribly familiar ring to it.

Not a good start to the first day of fall, or autumn as Caroline still liked to call it. They got up even though it couldn't have been more than five in the morning: plenty to do today.

They decided on a cooked breakfast.

And then, still hungry, a second one.

#

After breakfast Caroline went to let out the chickens. The trees beyond the fence caught her eye. The leaves – everything – looked so luminous, so intricate, so alive. As if she wanted it, somehow.

The berries she picked for wine each glowed with richly coloured translucent depths. She could have got lost in the deep pile of them in the basket. The salt she took to put in the Kim Chi became a magnificent oriental crystal edifice. She wanted to climb up it. The Paks had taught her how to make Kim Chi to preserve vegetables, a year ago. She missed them: they had since returned to newly reunited Korea. Their house still stood deserted – handed back to the bank but unsold.

In the afternoon she helped Tad saw wood, and after eating more supper than either would have thought possible they lit the wood-burner for the first time.

She leant against him in the big easy-chair. Her kind, handsome husband who listened when she had nightmares, and believed her. She smiled up at him and let her hand steal towards his. *I want to tell you... so much. I want to tell you... everything...*

#

A month and a day later a message arrived from their daughter.

#

Twelve mile limit. I'm free!
Wanda.

#

They broke out home-made champagne to celebrate.
On All-Saints' a message arrived from their son.

Senior Lecturer, History, Southampton!
Wanda arrived safely.
Andrzej.

#

They got out more home-made champagne. They added some of Tad's home-distilled vodka.

Caroline noticed her heartbeat misbehaving as they staggered upstairs two hours later. She'd have to ask Mazzi to check it over in the morning. He worked as a cardiologist and kept an E.C.G. machine in the house 'for emergencies only'. Fadida said Caroline's dream that had saved their roof meant they should always count a request from her as urgent if anyone asked.

Then she remembered that Mazzi, Fadida and their three children had left for Jordan earlier that year. Somehow they'd managed to keep it quiet until they'd boarded. The crew of the ship, being Russian, hadn't let Homeland anywhere near it.

#

"Oh Tad... I was paddling at Calshot Beach! It's where we used to go when I was a child. I miss... Each pebble was like a planet. You could explore them. I wonder what Andrzej's doing. I bet Wanda doesn't get rocks through her window for being a scientist, now."

"And being half-Polish –"

"And speaking a foreign language..."

She put a hand to her wrist.

"My pulse's playing up again. What are we going to do?"

#

"Bloody hell Tad they've banned contraception! Even the Pope's up in arms!"

"What?"

"It was on the radio just now. No-one admitted the real reason, of course."

Population 200 million, down another four hundred thousand since June...

"And there's been another shooting. University staff again: fifty!"

"Let me guess: all with –"

"Foreign surnames, Dr Zarczinski."

He smiled bitterly. "What did you say, Dr Zonderland?"

"D'you think it's because they're running out of non-white people to terrorise?"

She sat, and put her fingers to her wrist.

"Oh get us some more foxglove tea would you? It's happened again."

Tad brought the tea. And an idea.

"It's a fantastic idea, love. But what're we going to tell the Colonel?"

They sat in silence, gazing into the wood-burner's flames.

"Tad..."

Her voice became a whisper.

"It was him. In that terrible dream I had on the last night of summer. He's not just our local friendly 'Defense and Security' head – the Militia. He's in the Project."

Tad stared into the flames.

"All the things we've told him, over the years, when he comes round here first-footing for the New Year. Oh God, Tad, the genius of it! We've been to someone's party, we come back tired and... and the worse for wear like a pair of teenagers, and there I was thinking he was humouring me because I once told him we used to do first-footing in England! And he,"

Caroline paled.

"...asks us a load of questions."

"It's not that serious, love. Think 'conversation management'. He asks about our friends, about what we're up to: I parry, and you're usually wanting to talk about something else altogether, like chickens or poetry. I'd never have guessed the part about the Project, though. Not till that night–"

"Night? I didn't tell you till the morning."

Tad stared at the flames for a long time, before turning to his wife:

"I had the same dream. Down to the last detail. Oh, except without the part about hearts. And it was my left arm –"

"It's not fair joking about this, Tad!"

He tore off a scrap of paper from the pile near the stove, wrote on it and folded it.

"OK: what was the Colonel wearing?"

"A lab-coat. White. Grey collar. With a dark blue turtleneck underneath."

She unfolded the proffered piece of paper, read it and blanched.

They stared at each other. Neither knew how long for.

Finally Caroline put her hands to her mouth to hide a grin.

"Now it's you that's joking. Come on, what is it?"

"We're supposed to have forgotten about being given that stuff, aren't we? So it hasn't worked! We haven't bought anything unusual either."

"What about my idea? That involves buying something."

"I suppose it does, yes."

"It could even involve a bank loan. The biggest we can get, if we want to –"

"Is that allowed?"

"Depends which bank we use, I guess."

They refilled their glasses and talked some more about the Colonel, and about 'conversation management'.

#

"They've rounded up another lot of college loan debt people. Sending them to do nuclear clean-up this time. After that leak. It was on the news.

And an interview with some idiot whining about the fall in the number of kids who want to study for a degree."

"That makes sense."

"And they had an academic chap on who was talking about how it was impossible to organise an international conference these days, what with the 200-day visa application thing, and the vetting. He says from now on, there's an agreement, American academic conferences'll be held in Canada. Or Puerto Rico. I'm glad I'm retired now."

"Yes. Quantum Physics <u>probably</u> isn't what it was..."

"You're incorrigible, Tad!"

"Then don't incorrige me!"

#

On St Andrew's Day morning a message arrived from their daughter:

#

Job at Lloyds. Climate modelling, insurance. Settling-in grant for new immigrant!

Did Quarantine on IoW! Country now clear of Feline Flu. Pop. back up to 30 million.

Wanda.

#

In the afternoon, word arrived from their son:

#

Found out what you asked, about NHS.
Treatment still free if born in UK.
Andrzej

#

The chimes from the clock tower in town carried in the still, cool air.

"There it is: twelve midnight. Twenty twenty-six!"

Standing on the porch in front of the open door, they raised their glasses of home-made champagne:

"Happy New Year!"

"Absent friends!"

In the silence, the first snow began to fall. They stood and watched for a while, before returning inside and closing the door.

"Must be the only New Year in ages when we haven't got pie-eyed at somebody's party."

"Or stoned on that cake at Mazzi and Fadida's."

They heard the knock at the door.

"Just as well." Tad smiled.

"Happy New Year, Colonel! Come in!"

#

He crossed the threshold – handed Tad the bundle of wood, and Caroline the jar of salt. He noticed their hallway looked the same as ever: same old pictures and wall-hangings, rough wooden walls, nothing new here. Well, give it time. The bank loan was a good sign. He had a trick up his sleeve this year, as well as that good first question –

"Fancy some gluwein?"

He nodded his thanks as she passed him the hot glass cup with its silver holder. Caroline Zonderland: Englishwoman. Why's her surname Dutch? Meaning 'without a country'? He watched her pour some for Tad and some for herself. They went through and sat near the wood-burning stove.

He wasn't supposed to know what the word 'gluwein' meant. *Never mind: start the questions, Herz. It's what you're here for.*

"So: you guys makin' any good New Years' Resolutions this year?"

He noticed them glance at each other. It took him aback that Caroline spoke first.

"Actually, we have, and it's... a bit different from the usual. We've... had to borrow some money to do it –"

An abrupt halt as Tad flashed his wife a look to say, *you've said too much.* Well, he knew about the bank loan anyway. The Bank's records were a Security matter, after all. Didn't want anybody getting up to no good.

He noticed Caroline blush.

Gotcha.

He nodded for her to go on.

"You probably know, er, about my heart? It had to be repaired... in England when I was small. They always said it might need more done to it... as I got older."

And she's never taken it to a medic here in the States. That's no good...

"I've been using foxglove tea to keep it steady, but that's beginning not to work now. And it's dicey: you probably don't know but the therapeutic dose and the, er, danger line, they're not too far apart. So this year we're taking the plunge: I'm going to get one of those Enhanced Hearts put in."

"Aw, that's such good news! 'Cause I remember, you were trashin' them last year, sayin' they were no good for some reason of your own, and I got worried aboutcha."

"Really? I don't remember ever talking to you about such a thing!"

"Sure you did. You said they had 'privacy implications', with information 'bout your vital signs and location goin' everywhere."

He noticed her transient frown.

"Well, tough." She smiled. "I've had a change of heart!"

Limeys. Puns.

"Basically, I want to live beyond the age of sixty-five. Which is only next year, after all."

"Where ya havin' it done, if ya don't mind me askin'?"

"We haven't made our minds up yet. I need to do a bit of research. It used to be so easy with the 'net, but now..."

"You have to be loaded to afford it." Tad sighed.

He pondered the pros and cons of offering them the use of his home connection: pro, he'd know exactly what they were up to without having to rely on the poorly-maintained central databank. Con: he'd have to admit to being high enough up to have one at all. Plus, they'd be in his house: they might see stuff. He decided to stay <u>schtum</u> for the time being. See what transpired.

"More gluwein?"

He watched Caroline take the glasses through to the kitchen. She turned her back to refill them.

"Oh, I nearly forgot: I broughtcha something extra this year."

She set down her glass and took the large, soft, brown-paper parcel. She undid the string bow. He studied her reaction carefully as she pulled back the paper and the clean white stars looked up at her from their deep blue background.

She realises what it is... now.

She doesn't flinch: doesn't look ill-at-ease. Her face lights up.

"Oh that's fantastic, thank you! Is it for the front garden?"

"Sure."

"Do you know, I've always preferred it to ours. Crosses are so... cr –"

Shit: do they know?

"–uel."

"I can't remember if I toldya this last year, but I've applied to have my surname changed. You guys ever thoughta –"

"Oh! That's so sad. It's a nice name. It's German for Heart, isn't it?"

He stared at her face: his look that demanded an explanation.

"We learned foreign languages at school in England." She blushed. "That's how I know."

"Betcha miss that, don'tcha?"

"No I don't! It was a lot of hard work!" Her blush deepened. "Were your family from Germany?"

He could feel his face change colour. He'd wanted to ask them about their family: about their children. Do they miss them? Are they plotting to Return, to be near them? Scramming to England with that two hundred grand: private transfer. And not having to repay it. The new European banking laws allowed for that: have it declared an Odious Debt...

"Yes... yes they were. A long time ago now. How 'bout yours?"

"Flemish weavers. A... very long time ago now. Henry VIII let them stay: help the economy by making things from the wool that we - that England - had loads of at the time."

He didn't ask about Tad's family, because he already knew. Polish Home. Youngest partisan, known as 'the postman', could deliver any message, anywhere, empty-handed and unnoticed: anything, no matter how long, provided it had been recited in rhyme. Because 'the postman' was a girl: Tad's mother. Got caught out. Didn't talk. Four days. Rescued by the Hunters, Tad's father's gang.

Rescued from interrogation at the hands of Herz of the SS: his grandfather. Back home, everybody knew the name. Here, in the New World, he'd been hoping to be free of it. But last year's application to change it had been turned down...

He didn't want to ask any more questions.

"Well, guess I'd better hit the road."

#

"Progress report, Herz."

"Formula F5, you asked me to find a real toughie. I found 'em. Couple who're doing the self-sufficient thing, homestead, nearby me in New Hampshire.

"Took 'em less than three months to run up a $200,000 loan. Spendin' it on medics."

"Name?"

"Zarczinski. And Zonderland."

"A couple, with different names? They Homo?"

Herz grinned.

"She's a retired academic. Kept her name when she married. Lot of them do in Europe, 'pparently. He worked for the Feds and got himself a Psychology degree along the way."

"You sure they ain't figurin' on usin' the money for –"

"Returners? Can't be."

"How d'ya know for sure?"

"Passed the Flag Test. Flying colours."

#

The ocean stretched out before them: grey, austere; free. Like Caroline's eyes. Tad gazed at her as she watched the slim crescent of the extra sail uncurling into the West wind: the wind that would take them to Southampton, before the spring equinox gales got up.

"Well done about the flag. The cross bit was genius!" He put an arm round her shoulder. "Did you know that the German for swastika is –"

"Yes: I was trying to get the 'crooked' in but I couldn't think of a way that wasn't too obvious."

"Put him right off his stride!"

Tad leaned towards her,

"The look on his face: I bet he's got a family secret. I wish I knew."

"Probably best off not knowing. It was all a long time ago now. What, eighty years? And even if there is, it's not his fault."

Always rational: always the scientist. Even though the matter of her life's work didn't seem to behave that way: matter endowed with Strangeness, Top-ness; Charm ...

He followed her gaze out to sea. Did the waves on the ocean recall her work to her? Particles tracing out the patterns of ghostly waves: waves that didn't yet exist. As if those particles somehow knew the future. The possibility – barely touched upon yet – that this shadowy play may be at work in the mind, in consciousness itself. In those occasional haunting dreams of hers...

A boat came alongside. The Tannoy announced passenger roll call.

"Homeland. Time for a last bit of Conversation Management." Tad smiled.

"They should get a different name. Breach of the Trades Descriptions Act calling themselves 'Land' and coming and bothering us out here at sea. Like bloody pirates."

Everybody made their way below decks. It looked like over a hundred people, lined up before the Homeland team who swaggered about with their automatic weapons.

"How did it ever come to this?" Caroline whispered. "When the Government's always saying we're free, and then... It's like –"

"They're a law unto themselves, the Project, that's why. Homeland's kind of a part of them, now. It was already starting to get that way in the F.B.I. before I retired. Port authorities still hate them, though. That's why they can't check us as we board: have to resort to this."

He leaned in and added:

"And they hate people travelling overseas. Gives us <u>ideas</u>. Dangerous ideas, like, 'You don't need air-con in New Hampshire'."

Caroline smiled.

"Aarhus!"

A family stepped forward nervously.

"Reason for journey."

"Mother's funeral," said the woman. "Here are our tickets: outward, and back."

"Tad! They've got a polygraph! You know what my heartbeat's like: it's going to –"

"Daughter's wedding, remember? What mother isn't going to be all excited about that? Also explains the thirty Grand in bills: deposit for the first house. Come on: Conversation Management. You can do it."

The Homeland man bent down in front of the first family's smallest child,

"What's your name?"

"Aarhus, E!" announced the child.

"Well, Aarhus, E.: Can you tell me," he asked slowly, "When and where your grandmother's funeral is?"

"NO!!" the child clutched her teddy. "Ma said I'd be upset if... if..." She burst into tears.

And so it went on, through the alphabet: getting nearer and nearer.

Caroline smiled. But he noticed she was still blushing: it didn't look good.

"Zark... er,"

The Homeland agent indicated them with his semi-automatic.

"Them zee names!"

They stepped forward.

The ship's horn sounded.

Twelve mile limit!

The Captain came on the Tannoy.

"Ladies and Gentleman, members of the crew and," he paused, "any extra security staff who may be on board. We have now left United States Territorial Waters for the open ocean. The ship is under my direct jurisdiction, in accordance with International Law. I remind you all that the use or threat of use of firearms on board without my express permission constitutes Piracy and that," they could almost hear the smile, "we are sailing for England, under whose laws that particular crime is punishable by hanging."

"D'you know," Caroline smiled, "this might be the only time ever that I don't feel terrible about us reintroducing the Death Penalty?"

"Nor me about the ship's crew packing heat," Tad added with a grin.

#

He pulled up in the front yard. He noticed, before turning off the headlights, the immaculate covering of snow. No footprints. Well, of course: the Zees, as everyone round here called them, had gone away on vacation. Not a conventional vacation, no. Just got in the car and driven off to 'Oh, let's just see where we end up'. Good old-timers' road-trip. Most unlike them to even do that, all their friends said, but he knew the reason: F5, deep in their brain chemistry, working its magic. He smiled.

Why had he come here? To check out the story about the heart: was there any paper trail? Appointment letters pinned to the notice-board, meds on the kitchen counter.

He noticed the flag, hung in the front yard for all to see. Found himself trying the door before getting out his Universal Keys.

The door opened.

The hallway felt different, and not just because no fire burned, and no lights shone. It sounded less welcoming than he remembered.

He flicked a light-switch.

No power.

Only after returning to the Jeep to get his flashlight did he see what had changed in the hallway: the wall-hangings, and all the pictures, were gone.

He went through to the living room. No papers on the sideboard. None in the kitchen either – there had always been a huge pile there on the occasions when he'd called in before.

In all of the ground floor rooms, he found not a single sheet of paper: not even a till receipt or a bank statement – nada.

The stove gave it away. Black, curled sheets of ashes slept there. Everything had been burned. And with no computer in the house, that meant no records.

He knew what he would find on checking their bank files in the morning: they'd gone, and taken the money with them, to Poland, or England. British bank. He'd had to give ten-day notice to check the files.

He should have pressed them on how they felt about being thousands of miles from their children. Should maybe even have asked them what they thought of the Project: anything to draw them out.

He couldn't stand it – couldn't face failure.

He left the house.

As he crossed the garden, he noticed something white on the lowest corner of the flag. A note had been pinned there. An envelope, addressed to him.

He opened it and read, just four words:

We know your secret.

It was torture. Which one? Did they know what had been done to them? Or had they found out about his family's past? And they were such careful people. A blackmailer could easily be silenced, but not these. They'd have left details with a lawyer someplace: probably Poland, making the most of the language barrier. In any case they wouldn't be in it for the money: they were dissidents, driven by other goals.

He should have been able to persuade them to stay: to make them stay, and lure their children back. All four of them on F5, no longer dissidents. Happy, borrowing, spending. Helping the country keep going. Avoiding a sudden downturn.

Because he knew history.

He knew what had happened to his old country after a sudden economic downturn.

Knew, from his grandfather.

They'd started by picking on people with foreign surnames ...

C. L. Spillard

Benjamin Britten

UNNAMED ROAD, KYIVS'KA OBLAST

At the checkpoint to the Exclusion Zone
fledgling swallowswing on soft spring air,
officials demand passports and papers,
everybody makes an X, spread-eagled
at the machine testing contamination levels.
The only road signs are a sickly yellow
ionizing radiation hazard symbol, triangles
of black trefoil more like axes than trees.
Do not act as if it is an amusement park.
It is a place of nuclear disaster and remains
very dangerous, the warning states.
Although, hell, there's already been art
raves here in the cleared square at Pripyat,
roses open like eyes in too bright light
between the grids on concrete paving.
Mutations only show at microscopic scale.
A brisk wind shifts across the green
spurt of poplars. Birches and firs growing.

Spurt of poplars. Birches and firs growing.
A brisk wind shifts across the green.
Mutations only show at microscopic scale.
Between the grids on concrete paving
roses open like eyes in too bright light
raves here in the cleared square at Pripyat.
Although, hell, there's already been art.
Very dangerous, the warning states.
It is a place of nuclear disaster and remains.
Do not act as if it is an amusement park
of black trefoil more like axes than trees,
ionizing radiation hazard symbol, triangles
The only road signs are a sickly yellow.
At the machine testing contamination levels
everybody makes an X, spread-eagled
officials demand passports and papers,
fledgling swallowswing on soft spring air,
beyond the checkpoint to the Exclusion Zone.

Briar Wood

DESERT
Cairo 1942

This patchwork tent lashed to a jeep
with its meccano mess of bolts and wires
is no shelter at all. One single shell
could blast the lot to buggery and Smudger,
Spud, Vic, Jock and the Professor
would be on their own. An ocean of sky
between them and the base.

My dad looks young – the moustache
and pipe can't have fooled anyone.
He's the age I was when I spent
the summer on a Corfu beach,
mostly stoned, head full of Sartre.
And here he is, guiding packs of fighters
down the desert corridor into Alamein.

The air is hot with diesel. In the distance
tanks skim the desert, muzzles bristling,
sand spraying from their side skirts.
Inside the tent the monitor winks and beeps.
Let me help, I say. He turns and nods
as if he knows me. He can't, of course,
but why do I think he's guessed?

You could sharpen this, he says,
handing me a blunt stub of pencil
and an Air Force issue penknife.
I bite my lip and concentrate,
precise in the rate of my paring.
He watches dots sink from the screen
and scribbles numbers on his pad.

Important, must fly. He gathers his papers
and exits through the canvas flap
leaving heat and silence.
I flick the pencil shavings from my sleeve.
Is he coming back? Of course not.
I run my thumb over the lead – needle sharp –
and lay it on the table by his still warm pipe.

David Lukens

Dark Valley

Trees stand their ground –
beaconic, pulsating with seasons,
growing the length of a waka.
Night rains break the drought.

Light lozenges and starblasts
in the electronic pā, ūkaipō,
the distant river's whisper.
Papatūānuku on snooze alert.

Why does the word *dark*
have such negative connotations?
Dim, shady, shadowy, murky.
And that's just for a start.

Terrible events take place
in the light of day –
in words it hurts to speak;
to say dark that way is a cliché.

Trying waitematā, or kōpuni,
or pukepoto like a tui wing isn't hard.
Darkling can be affectionate –
loving even, like dorcha and tewl.

Watch the logging trucks lit up
like a settlement in Siberia,
graunch diesel-drunk uphill,
beyond the road to the general hospital.

Briar Wood

CHECKLIST

Think of a country
that breathes carefully,

of faces daily ageing
a thousand years,

of questions
booby-trapped,

of smiles
a regime property,

of blows
as the best to hope for,

of disappearance
a currency of protest,

of escape
as a hole in the ground.

Then pouring yourself
from your immunity,

forget it's you or them
and feel reality.

Then name your loved ones
without crying.

Gordon Scapens

THEY DON'T TELL YOU

They don't tell you you must cross the desert
        before you find the man with the papers.

They don't tell you the man with the papers
        wears dark glasses and has a woman he treats badly.

They don't tell you the man in the dark glasses
        will demand extra money for your wife and family.

They don't tell you you'll sail in a fishing boat
        with hundreds of others.

They don't tell you the fishing boat has no bunks,
        rotting food and not enough water.

They don't tell you the captain wants the last of the money
        that you'd set aside to start your new life.

They don't tell you the crew will beat you
        and lock you in the holds.

They don't tell you about the pitching and rolling in the dark,
        the sound of retching, the smell of urine and vomit.

They don't tell you that as you near land
        you will be forced on to rafts and abandoned.

They don't tell you about the panic,
        the struggling, the choking, the drowning.

They don't tell you that, if you survive,
        no country will want you.

Alice Harrison

There'd be nothing from the layby café now. Only its kitchen fan worked on, wafting greasy air into his cab. Bren stilled the engine and exited the artic. He'd have rather unloaded tonight but, with the haul to Esbjerg and from Immingham, he'd done his ten. Bren wouldn't make the city and couldn't stretch the tacho.

"How's it going, Seamus?"

He'd joined a colleague beside the single streetlight, in front of the café that fronted only grain fields, glowering gold in the late evening sun. August! He could hear blackbirds rapping in spiked bursts, could glimpse bugs and bats grimly courting.

"Be better if United had won," Seamus replied.

"Wouldn't City have lost then?"

"The disallowed goal! You didn't see it, Bren? Look."

Seamus proffered his smartphone. Bren's mind was buffering when a reefer parked at a neighbourly distance. Glaring from its cab was Matty's glowing crucifix. He'd got the cross in a 'pope-shop' in Italy. The hell-red bulbs were his twist on it, an unsettling sight on an unlit A-road. Matty was a laugh. His air-horn – bought in Spain – could play La Bamba. Bedouins, they were. Or he and Matty were. Seamus wasn't a continental driver.

"All right Bren, Seamus?"

Matty had joined them below the light, switched on now, a cone of tartrazine. He was running a shaver round his jaw.

"Ah, living the dream," Seamus said.

Bren turned on him. "Having work enough to fend off the wolf, and no boss on your back in the cab, no bosses anywhere if you obey the rules of the road, and no IEDs there to wake you – which bit makes you smirk, Seamus?"

"Down, boy! You been od'ing on Jeremy Vine again?"

"I hate that saying too," Matty said, pocketing the shaver, "How defeated we are, how disappointing life is!"

"Defeated and disappointed every Saturday,' Seamus said. "There's no justice. The disallowed –"

"Me, I'm dreaming the life."

"And yet here we all are driving wagons, Matty. I'm off to water the wheat," Seamus said, holding his gut like a football, the nearest he got to playing lately.

These were never the conversations Bren imagined having after a day alone in the cab, Gwen's diamond earrings swinging from the visor, unpicking the sunlight. They hadn't done rings or bands. He still wore one gold stud.

Matty eyed Bren. "*Are* you all right? Not that he's right. Silly sod! You'd never know he had a wife, two kids. All you get is balls balls balls."

"Yes but –"

"Reminds me of what my old dad told me when he was propped up in the Royal dying, when I was daft enough to ask him what it was all about, what it all meant."

"Hard to be smart in that situation, Matty."

"So it's very early or very late and we're very alone. I ask dad and he says, 'It's all balls'. My mum, me, my own boy – balls."

"*What?*"

"Aren't I glad I asked."

"That's the drugs," Bren said. "He *was* on morphine or something?"

"Yes, but no. He meant it. Never meant anything more."

"Maybe he'd had enough, Matty. The wife spent her last weeks in a hospice. Lovely room, lovely Moors view. And I watched Gwen turn her face to the wall."

"Sorry, I didn't know."

"All I'm saying is, maybe it's not for us to say. They're the ones dying."

"Maybe," Matty shrugged. "The machine's on, fancy an espresso?"

Before the daylight went Bren walked his trailer, checking the tyres and the tilt cord. A ribby Dalmatian cross loped up and sniffed round. Bren bent to distract it and spotted a collar and tag. Some wolf! "Now then, Inky."

But the dog had already bridled. It barked at Bren's rear door.

"Inky! Leave it, son." Bren's brother truckers materialised. "Dogs normally like me."

"You carrying bones?" Seamus smiled.

And then there was a banging inside the trailer to accompany the barking outside it.

"Christ, you haven't?" Matty said.

Bren couldn't prevent the noise, nor his friend from cracking open the rear door. Two scrub-bearded brown men shook themselves out of it.

"Down! Sit down!" Seamus barked, and not to Inky, whose swatches of black and white were swapping in the half-light.

The clandestines respected the verge and sat blinking on the warm tarmac. Over their heads, the unblinking truckers eyed each other, until Seamus fished out his smartphone.

"Who you calling?"

"Proper coppers then Border Force, isn't it?"

"Don't talk balls," Matty replied.

"Quiet!" Seamus said and smacked Inky across the nose, who quieted. The chill cycle of Matty's reefer carried across the layby.

"There're two-thou fines if Bren didn't know about this pair. There's prison if he did."

"Bastards," Seamus swore at the men. "Where are you from? Got any papers? Speak English?"

But the two were blank, offering no eye contact, not even to each other. One extended his legs and scratched his left ankle, the other pulled at his stubble.

"Hablas español? Parli italiano?" Matty tried.

Nothing.

"Bloody hell, Bren. Say something if they won't."

"Iraq. They're from Iraq."

"My apologies, Inky," Seamus said. "I was there the first go round. Let's get them sent back."

"You going to testify in Bren's defence?"

"Sod that! He says they were hitchhiking."

"And they *don't* say he was smuggling?" Matty said. "Let's not let them. Let's have our own say."

"What?"

"Not like a trial. No guilt or innocence. Just facts. They tell their stories. We say if they stay or go. My sister-in-law does it for the Home Office in Liverpool. Let's save her a job."

"And who translates?"

"He does," Bren said, indicating the younger Iraqi.

"Water," he replied.

"It's always water," Seamus said, "when you're made to sit in the dirt with nothing."

A bottle was brought and some cab-scraps for Inky. The clandestines drained the liquid then looked at Matty, who crouched to their eye-level in the sallow spotlight. Night had fallen beyond it.

"Which part of Iraq are you from?"

"What difference does *that* make?" Seamus interrupted.

"You remember your tour, or ever watch the news – the bit prior to the footy results? There's Sunni and Shia Muslims and they were mullering each other long before they got round to us."

The younger Iraqi nodded. "We are Shia. Saddam is not our president. When you British win, I am interpreter."

"And where's this?"

"In Basra."

The older Iraqi nodded at that.

"Basra *is* Shia," Matty said, feathering his smartphone. "Port city, full of Bedouins once."

"I am not conscript, my uncle is not having the moustache."

"The – ? Doesn't matter. What happened?"

"There is new enemies. Insurgency, Daesh. I am on the list of interpreters. My uncle, the list of teachers."

"*Teachers*?"

"To win in Saddam's Iraq, you join the party and have the moustache. But everyone who is not winning is making a list."

"Google's got something about teachers being shot," Matty said.

"Outside the ministry for teachers," the nephew nodded.

"Yes! I mean, *Jesus*."

"To interpreters they do worse. And then you British forget us. We move to Najaf but the lists do not forget."

"Didn't we help you?"

The nephew smiled. "There is the LESAS who come to Britain. I am not on *this* list."

No one fact-checked that. No one stopped the younger Iraqi from rising.

"I will have justice, Insha'Allah! Do you British have justice?"

Inky was barking a fraction before Seamus.

"Hold on, pal! Cameron's as much my man as Saddam was yours. The government don't speak for me. I'm the people. I say who's legit and who's a dirty liar."

"*Kafir!*"

"Shut it and sit down."

But he didn't do either until his uncle addressed him in Arabic and the truckers in English.

"My nephew is sorry. He is young. He is tell the truth."

Inky subsided as the younger Iraqi crouched, itching his left ankle again.

"It's true," Matty read, "like Churchill and the *Narzees*. Daesh is a diss for Isis, and they do not like the Shia."

"He's legit. They both are. Which is what I was told," Bren said.

"The uncle says the nephew isn't a liar," Seamus snorted. "Or they're both liars. Why's he pretend he couldn't speak English?"

"It is better," the older Iraqi replied. "We is driving round like children, mafia to mafia, by mafia maybe. No *refuge*. I am listen. What is your nature? What do you do with us?"

"We're not criminals," Seamus said. "You are. And Bren is. What are you playing at, mate?"

"Gwen was head of year, good salary, no pension yet," Bren replied. "The wolf's at the door."

"And if you don't show up in Leeds with these two, any comeback?"

"No, they paid in advance."

"So Bren's in the clear and they're both legit, Seamus. So we set them loose, dial 999 anonymously. We're miles from anywhere. They're going nowhere bar the back of a Black Maria."

"Do we count to a hundred before calling the coppers?"

"The fact is they're the same as us. Bedouins don't do jail, there's freedom or a fine, and they paid in advance."

"You spiking your espressos, Matty? They're legit, or they're illegit enough to fool three thick truckers. Maybe *they're* Isis. Let's get them sent back."

The nephew said, "You British –"

Matty cut across him. "Where are *you* from, Seamus?"

"Manchester, me and Bren both."

"And your family?"

"Same: mammie's from Levenshulme, da's from the Emerald Isle, why?"

"So it's all right for your dad and for Bren's but not for these two? Migrant, refugee, same sodding difference. The world's unfair. People are forever on the move, dreaming the life." Matty regarded the layby, the Iraqis, and the other truckers. Streetlight yellowed all their skins, though the sky was brightening once more. "If you could just tell us why you and your nephew would want to be *here*, because I have no idea these days."

"The days, I do not see. I am in the truck. But the truck is not a bomb, and nowhere is desert, even the air is smelling green, and the nights I do see is not dark. Never dark. Light is like this, like honey."

Like –?

The younger Iraqi was standing again. Was bending. Was flashing a knife.

The others retreated, barring Inky. He started barking and only stopped when the nephew's sharp fist franked his head. Inky bowed into his own blood. Which, unquiet, reached out to the men. The younger Iraqi stabbed the verge to clean his blade then brought its tip to Bren's glinting ear lobe. "*Kafir.*"

But Bren was remembering the rounds of clinics, the driving home all hours with Gwen deep in the back seat, the night deep in her. He shook his head despite the knife.

"Just piss off, can't you?" Seamus said, nodding at his wagon and offering his keys to the clandestine.

The blade weighed the sun before reaping the keyring. Each trucker was made to empty his pockets onto the tarmac. The nephew smashed their phones and took nothing but his knife to the tires of the other wagons.

"*Nice* family," Seamus said.

The older Iraqi was pulling at his beard. He bent to retrieve the shaver, hailed his compatriot and joined him. The uncle indicated the sky. Both clandestines faced southeast and bowed from the waist and the older struck the younger on the head. He fell beside his knife.

The truckers ran over.

"Is he –?" Bren stopped.

But the nephew was breathing as lightly as the uncle was heavily.

"You're never related," Seamus smiled.

"We make a story. I am Ali. He is Kasim."

"What now?" Matty asked Seamus.

"Kasim wants it worse than any of us, so we leave him here, agreed?"

The other three nodded.

"After we bury the dog and before I drive you wherever, Ali, breakfast is on us. *Qahwa* all round. Shame about the bacon, they do a mean sarnie."

For the Oasis café was opening.

IN THE FIRELIGHT

That night you seemed taller, striding
sure-footed through the cabbage stalks
in damp November darkness,
fleetingly half-lit by bonfire flames,
flares of matches, falls of silver sparks.

We stood back, watched you
absorbed in the tasks: tossing branches,
raking ashes, lighting touch papers
in sequence, choreographing the show.
A rocket's starburst lit up your face

and I saw that young man, bobbing
in dark diesel sea, off the coast
at Alexandria, lit up by searchlights
from a rescue ship, the souvenirs
fast sinking to the ocean floor.

The final firework exploded – a volley
of shrapnel starbursts: I pictured
the pitted scars across your thighs
and noticed firelight flickering
in her eyes as she looked on, smiling.

Marion Ashton

BRONTË IN ALEPPO

A Syrian schoolgirl, trapped in her cellar, blogged that she was enjoying reading her small library of classic English novels.

The water bottles are back and full, thank God,
so we can sip and plash our fingers, wash out our rags.

For the third time this year Jane leaves the ghosts
of Gateshead Hall, the room they shut her in, for moorland air,

false hope, Lowood's disease, the cant of power that crushes everything.
Beyond the lightning-sculpted trees, a limestone ridge,

a male world waits to trouble her blood with unspoken tragedy.
Faded tapestries and polished walnut, an architecture of prose.

The house will burn. Madness brings it down,
hide it behind however many doors you will,

but Jane will see it through.
Love, like death, cannot be locked away.

A blade of sun knifes through the grill
and the impossible becomes fact.

Rochester holds his newborn, sees his child through healing eyes
and then I'll start again at Chapter One.

Martin Reed

WE NEED TO TALK ABOUT BRANWELL

He obliterated all traces
of his face with crude brushstrokes,
turning himself into a column.

Three sisters are arranged around it,
clad in the same degree of sobriety.
These disquieting muses

out-stare the prodigal brother,
poet, painter and writer of sagas
more fantastical than *Game of Thrones*.

Over time, transparency of paint
is beginning to reveal the lines and curves
of his glittering image.

Mesmeric. Beyond ironic.
Chief Genius Branwell of Glass Town
stealing the limelight.

Note.- The Pillar Portrait of the Bronte Sisters painted by Branwell Brontë hangs in the British Museum.

Miriam Sulhunt

CAWOOD

Kings and Queens, Lords and Knights,
Bishops, a Cardinal, pass through this gate.
Ostlers run to take the horses;
a yard-man sweeps and shovels.

From the inner court he comes,
expansive, cunning, genial,
the Archbishop, primed,
wielding the knife of protocol.

His palace, his castle, his right to crenellate
here in the North. The King his guest,
others, supplicants. Tomorrow, the feast.

Tables bow beneath the weight of meat,
of trenchers, of syllabubs, of flagons and fruit.
He plies his guests with wine, with sweetmeats, delicacies,
peacock, swan, quail, according to rank – he, himself, holds back.

For who knows what gems may slip from a tipsy mouth,
what secrets, what drunken generosity,
what shifts in the balance between
one carving and the next?

Tomorrow, or the next day, the cavalcade rolls on
to prayers in the city, the crowds pressed in.
A royal progress to sniff out treason,
re-inforce alliance, hug the archbishop close.

Old arm-wrestlers, tight in each other's grip,
eyes alert for the flash of treachery
or the bright royal axe.

John Gilham

SHE ASKS A QUESTION

If in a poem there happens
to be a blue door,
is it just a blue door
or something else? So that all
I can see now are blue doors,
or parts of doors, each behind
another. I think they have
panels of some kind, they are
standard door-sized doors.
All of them lumbering, footless
towards me. Won't speak.

Not least of my problems, I have
only limited power to visualise
(faces, objects, places, tend
to elude me) and these doors
are starting to worry me now.
As is the question.
I'm suddenly wary. What
do you mean by door
in this context?
Precisely what led you
to think it was blue?

Carolyn Oulton

THREADS

Let me set this down before I lose
the thread. The lady at her loom,
the mirrored room, the parable
that Mary, penitent, would tell:
a seamstress went out to sew and where
the tears appeared she darned them well.

Or, besieged among the olive trees
whose trunks, wind-wrung, fray to grey-
green shelter like wool unspun, all under
a robe-blue sky, the warlord's wife
unpicks and sews, unpicks and sews,
drawing the thread that hauls her husband home.

We who spin a tale to stay the blow,
who do not wield but weave, weighing each stitch, each word,
against the heft of Fate, slip through
the needle's eye where those who sow
discord dare not go. Our Lady
of the Needle and the Loom defend us.

Susan Wallace

I found it hard to visualise two meters, thinking instead of gas, electric, water, or parking, so I climbed into my rusty first car that I hadn't driven since the mid-80s. It was full of gas and spiders, and started first time. The city had been repainted overnight by De Chirico, with no movement but a distant train, and parking bays unoccupied save for a statue of reclining Ariadne. I pulled up on the pavement, tied a thread to my wrist so as not to lose myself in the unfamiliar absences, and walked north, hoping to meet erstwhile companions. Instead, I found nothing but abandoned phones, with unsupported apps and mistyped passwords, and mounds of desktop pcs sucking electricity for no practical ends. In a cream K6 callbox, a phone was ringing, so I wiped it carefully with methylated spirit and answered. Ariadne's voice dripped like water into my ear, and I spied her through the smeared panes, Nokia 1011 pressed to her cheek, fluttering along an avenue of sightless storefronts. The thread was broken, but she invited me to meet her, though she insisted we remain four cubits apart.

Oz Hardwick

YOUNG WOMAN, POMPEII

She died, we were told, of asphyxiation.
You can see the way the sleeve ruched
around her left elbow
as her hand covered her mouth
, little protection, she knew,
from the poison air.

In Naples it's so hot we're cracking.
In alleys the scooters threaten an inglorious end
and the cupids are caught in nets.
I don't talk to you all the way to the castle.
I'm spitting ash.

From the walls we see Vesuvius.
I say god, the sea, and you touch
your neck where it's burned.
We turn our backs to the volcano.
We hold hands and I can breathe again.
The harbour is that sort of blue.

When they pour plaster
into the space I have occupied,
they will find the sleeve ruched
around my left elbow.
I will be covering your mouth
, little protection, I know,
from the poison air.

Kathryn Haworth

EUTERPE

These inland waters, trawled nightly yet for jetsam
and jewels, for treasures which elude, lately yield
little, worthless washed-up clobber spawning small
fry like this which flip and pirouette away, forgotten
even as she shakes sleep from her eyes. Yet night by night
she baits her line and sets her net again; again

she sharpens spear with anger, her line
she has ripped from a lyre, her net stripped
from the fallen. Eyes pressed tight, she watches
for the glitter of lost shoals, one mind, flitting,
turning; stalks the leviathan lurking solitary,
circling, out there beyond the shallows.

These lakes have seasons like the moon:
pooled in perfect circles to the earth's curve
or spilled over, showing only the bright sickle licking
at the well's rim. In landlocked dawn she recalls
how once she stood, supplicant among the irises, hands
open like leaves of water lilies, waiting for the rain.

Susan Wallace

PAUSING FOR ORANGES

She puts the flowers in the bin
        with the cake,
sits down in the kitchen,
        lets rind harden on the floor.
She feels lust rise in her purse
        and checks her bank account.
Scum settles in the sink.
        She pours herself a glass of wine,
throws a cloth over his photo,
        pulls her cardy round.

She searches cupboards
        for bread and marge,
pours gravy on an empty plate.
        Pausing after washing,
she looks in the mirror, catches
        her eye in the distance,
in an orchard, pruning oranges.
        She lifts her glass to the future,
takes the scarf from her head,
        and circles naked.

Mike Alderson

SISYPHUS

Rolling this stubborn boulder up this hill
I have driven myself half mad.
Call it a monomania if you will
but I am like a bulldog: once I bite
my jaw will not unclench until the teeth
are broken or the bone is bitten through.

I've felt its weight bear down against my back,
spat gristle and blood onto the stone,
ground the grit of failure in my joints,
and each day the fickle sun
has left me to my labours in the dark,
and still I have gone on,
clenching my heart into a fist against
the freezing grip of fear

until he rose again behind my back
and smiled upon my labours as before,
thawed my heart with visions of the future,
warm homecomings and accomplishments.
My heart has waned and waxed with moons,
died in winter, been reborn in spring,
chained to the wheel of the seasons
as I am hand-cuffed to this stubborn stone.

Sometimes a vision comes to me at night.
I stand upon the mountain's knuckled crest.
From heaven there falls a fountain of light,
and by it I am cleansed and blessed,
and it lifts away my pain.

I wake to feel the dirt beneath my feet,
my limbs burning and, ahead, the mountain
rising until it disappears in mist.

Taliesin Gore

When the light comes, the years won't keep still, and I find myself barefoot on Salisbury Plain. Thunder rolls, but there will be no rain. There are not even clouds, and even the notion of weather is a stranger. Away to the north, bushes are on fire, but sooner or later one always reaches the sea. The sky is full of myths and sketches from childhood books, a dot-to-dot of hunters, dogs and tangled webs. A yelp cuts the ground neatly to its beating beating beating heart, and I place my palm flat on the grassy, glassy wound. I fall asleep in the midday sun, but there is no distinction, though when I wake up my clothes are patterned with tyre tracks and I have framed certificates for achievements I'd never even considered. My lips are alive with straw-coloured wine, my backpack is full of Arthurian legends, and my hands are gold with blown dust. The years stack tight like a conjuror's cards, and I pull love by its ears from a silk top hat. It was always hidden there, but it still feels like magic.

Oz Hardwick

REVIEWS

Layers **by Clint Wastling**
Maytree Press
ISBN 978-1-9160381-8-9 £7.00 32pp

Clint Wastling has brought out his first collection, a slim volume of poetry that explores one of his constant interests: the layers under our feet; the layers under our skin. My formal archaeological education began with Geology 101, but started with collecting rose quartz (sharing my name!) and included a brief foray into rock-tumbling. Even driveway gravel shone with a grave lustre after being ground by increasingly finer grits. The constant grumblings eventually proved too much for mother; the tumbler vanished; my love of rocks has remained.

Clint's surf is the rock grinder here, placing us seaside, searching for ammonites as waves are "Uniformly attacking, grinding the applauding pebbles" (from 'Fossil'), one of my favourite images in the book: both sound and postcard.

Wastling explores the depths of Earth's layers as well as those of humankind. Perhaps it takes a scientist to lovingly examine both. He has a natural focus on family – we write what we know intimately - but also turns his geologist's gaze onto the folly of unmitigated global warming, our ruin of the natural world, and our collective refusal to address either. 'Poison' uses his sharpest pickaxe:

> "but here nothing lived except
> the farmer spraying winter wheat:
> pesticide, herbicide, fungicide."

'Belshazzar's Feast' pillories those in power who refuse to make any provision for our looming climate tragedy:

> "without air he cannot breathe,
> without water what use is wealth?"

His first poem, 'Lazy Shaving' is a cracker: one I know well as I submitted it for consideration for a well-known prize. In this sharp memory poem he recalls his father shaving; his own early attempts; his own ageing face, now in the mirror of adult life. His father visits us again in 'Bricklayer': "He could halve a brick with one rap of the trowel"; we meet his son, searching for fossils in 'Collecting Ammonites'. Wastling brings us portraits of mum in 'Sorting'. His wife is with him throughout this polished collection: the 'we' beside him in San Nicolo, along the Cote Vermeille, or viewing manatees in Florida. But family is mentioned only as part of a view to the larger picture. Wastling grounds himself, then gazes outward.

The natural world that grows above the rocky strata are also examined, be they waterfalls, islands, or the "quiet downs" in 'Avebury'. The layers Wastling explores are based on geological time and measured in millennia, but also by the human scale of decades. The book is marginally let down, but only slightly, by a few editorial quibbles (grumbles the editor) but it hardly detracts. I highly recommend this collection.

Rose Drew

John Dust, poems by Louise Warren, illustrations by John Duffin
V. (2019)
ISBN 978-1-9165052-8-5   £6.50
23 pages of poetry, 7 pages of black & white ink drawings.

Poetry comes from a deeply personal inner landscape. But sometimes external geographies play a powerful role too.

Enter *John Dust* – the riveting personification of Louise Warren's native Somerset. Dust feels dangerous, fascinating, unstable, yet deeply rooted. Warren has given us a Green Man for the modern age. Prepare to be charmed, hoodwinked, even seduced by Dust, who is:

". . . narrow as a pipe, face like a clay bowl
choked-up, stony-broke
chest blown open like a sunset . . .
coat stuffed with apples
coat stuffed with horsehair, tied round with sail rope
coat bursting open, burst out the linings
sodden green ditches, pricked through with heron,
pierced through with willow, bloody and wasted . . ."

His landscapes entwine us in their smells and sounds, their atmospheres and memories, like lovers:

" . . . Deep inside the bathroom I undress myself for you,
John Dust.
Down to the sedge and water, down to the beak of me,

Sharp in the reed bed, down to the hidden.
I strip the light from my skin until I am overcast,
Become cloud cover . . ."

Warren's imagery is lively and surprising, her rhythms inventive, with a sure use of repetition. Sometimes the pamphlet reads like a song. Sometimes it's emotional. Sometimes, playful. Always it relishes the vibrancy of words.

". . . the sky rusting over, smashed with egg yolks,
water as mirror, water as leather, water as smoke, as trick,
a light under the door."

John Dust poems rub shoulders with others that reflect the surreal, the uncanny edge to life – and death. 'Woman with small dog' tells of a 1,700 year old burial find in the Museum of Somerset. In others, Warren turns herself into a bird or a fox; finds meaning in the death of a fly:

"How beautiful and delicate he is in death
laid out on the white afterlife
like a god, a fly on the sill
in a tapestry of cup rings."

She tips her hat to Elliot in 'East Coker', and in a series of five poems 'The Parish Magazine', offers hilarious thumb-nail portraits of village life. '5 Riddles' challenges the reader to look under the bonnet of each poem for its double meaning (Spoiler alert: answers on page 30!)

Perhaps most moving of all, a nine line poem inspired by finding her late father's 1930s OS map, shows Warren at her most observant and understated. Could John Dust himself be an echo of what she hopes to find again? Landscapes, old maps – these are the tracks we follow when seeking things lost to us.

"some kind of weather is trapped here – damping, a cloud
from the 30s, pressed onto the page – vapour thin fog expanding
–

some kind of man is trapped here – his back to me smoking – "

Claire Booker

Restless Voices by Alan Price
Caparison 2020
ISBN 978-199937-466-2   £8.00 pp 52

We are advised not to judge a book by its cover, but what about by its title? *Restless Voices* is a pretty accurate description of Alan Price's latest collection, and as such a good guide to what the reader can expect.

The work is varied in method, style and outcome. Often the poems feel like interesting experiments being played out for the reader – and if we adopt the right perspective then we can be enthused and intrigued by the possibility afforded by playing with language.

An experimental landscape is set-up by Price himself, with the inclusion of two conversational treatises on the work included. The introductions are informative and certainly give the reader a way into the work, but should the poems need this much assistance? I certainly appreciate the fact that Price is sharing the process that he has adopted; it provides an insight into how a writer is operating to a degree that is refreshing.

The first sequence in *Restless Voices* is called 'Wholeness is a Problem' and it is in preparation of this section, that Price is at his most explanative. "You need to apply some basic, but not inflexible, rules", he writes in relation to cut-up poetry which is the method used for this sequence. Here we have twenty poems "that have evolved out of the letters of famous poets". Price reveals more of how he set about working on the sequence, "Sometimes I capitalise a letter or make it lower case". All of this appeals to one involved with writing (are all readers of poetry also writers?), and I'm sure those unfamiliar with the technique will gain from the introduction.

The cut-up approach is applied to letters written by poets. I'm sure many will have their own feelings about the merits of cut-up poetry; I think I'd mark myself as ambivalent, and so the work is already going to have to work hard. The poets and letters selected range from Aleksander Blok (writing about the revolutionary power of theatrical farce) to Wilfred Owen writing to his mother. I think Alan Price is right to offer up the idea that "there are always alternative options and choices: further cut-ups to be attempted and democratically shared". Thus, whilst giving himself a bit of a get-out clause, Price does make clear that this is just one way, his way, of playing the game – more players are cordially invited. The exercise, and I call it that deliberately, does stir my curiosity, perhaps even enough to try my own version.

I can't fathom the esoteric choices of some subjects in this series, and it may help if I knew more about some of the writers/recipients, but Price does give enough context as a footnote to give the poems shape. Speaking of which, I haven't yet got to grips with the formatting of the Larkin piece – a deliberate bit of concrete poetry that puzzles me.

However, I don't think Price would mind a bit of puzzlement from the reader. After all he refers to this sequence as "tampering" and sets us up for more playfulness in the introduction to the section called 'Solutions' (he is teasing us). Here he describes two of the poems as "a bit of mischief concerning bureaucracy"; these particular poems being a kind of cut-up poem about treatment in a hospital.

The humour is evident in this section, 'Solutions', and Price is happy not to take himself too seriously. The spin on jargon in a hospital is good fun and reads like a nightmare handbook,

> C) trust hospital shortages
> creating 'best in class' environmental junk
> hospitality cleans family food
> for charges and faults call a 3677

(from the poem, Privately, Trust Your Hospital)

Whilst the poems may not take themselves too seriously, it is only because of an ear for line endings and emphasis that Price is able to sustain some of the work – his skill should not be missed under the cover of subject matter.

Later in the collection comes more overt comedy in the form of two dramatic monologues. What I found most interesting in these was the way in which the female subjects were used to explore male perceptions. 'She Searched For A Ghost Writer' is told by a lady from Thailand, but it is the men she encounters, "God, these novelists, insurance men and bankers. All spoilt babies in the end," that we learn most about – a deft and scathing look at how men can behave. The two monologues would take flight as performance pieces, I suspect.

Among the cut-ups, monologues and translations (now you see why the book is called 'Restless Voices') are some 'straight' poems. I think 'Director's Nightmare' is a terrific poem that details the terrors of a film director at sea and under threat in the age of digital cinema. There is invention in the imagery, "Celluloid organs squirming", and such lines as "nerves a jangle of panic and noir" demonstrate that Price is perfectly capable of writing a fine poem of his own – no cut-up required.

An enjoyable ride is provided by these voices, and I think you just have to embrace the book with an open and exploratory frame of mind. This is not a typical collection of poetry; the writer shows you what goes on behind the curtain for a start. There is a touch of the workshop about things – but that's no bad thing – here is a set of poems that will send you down all kinds of new avenues, and that must be a good thing – particularly if you are a writer who reads poetry.

Neil Elder

Heft by **David J. Costello.**
Red Squirrel Press 2020
ISBN 978-1-913632-00-7   £10.00, pp76

We, like everything else that has life, did not ask to be born and endure what our inner and outer selves are often exposed to. Ancestral memory, loss in all its forms, hardship, the weather's machinations, increasing bureaucracy and other changes out of our control, especially war, when:

> 'we are here as on a darkling plain
> Swept with confused alarms of struggle and fight,
> Where ignorant armies clash by night!'
> ('Dover Beach', Matthew Arnold)

Just like the prescient and empathic Arnold, David J Costello's uniquely tuned antennae (as those of his beloved butterflies) delivers in this remarkable collection, equally meaningful aspects of our and other species' existence, with affection, awe and insight. A nature lover, with two successful pamphlets published, Costello's latest, vivid, heartfelt poetry, is epitomised by his first poem, the eponymous 'Heft' which takes us and certain breeds of sheep from 'the hoarse voice of the heather' to where 'Every lamb is impregnated with its map' and how 'their internal compass tugs them back to their heritage of rock. The heather's cackle and the milky white cartography of snow.'

So eloquently life-affirming (despite their likely ultimate fates) this was awarded second prize in the International Welsh Poetry Competition in 2018, while the poet's equally memorable 'Horseshoe Bat' had won it in 2011:

> 'It must have been a keen blade
> that eased you from night's heart.
> God's own shrapnel
> creasing the dark,
> Your convulsing fragment
> pressure-cracking the brittle black
> like ice.'

This wide-ranging collection also shows a refreshing lack of both egotistical navel-gazing and obscurantism. What Costello sees, feels, remembers and imagines is what you get. Powerful and unique observations together with insight makes his words unforgettable, as in 'Rowan.'

> 'Immersed in the cursed
> cut of cold air
> your tortured fossil
> unfurls its bony fan

in a carcass of
rock-wrought coral.'

Here is a tree, highlighted and regenerated by words, while

'The world hammers past
leaving you to bruise
in the blush of your shed berries.'

Costello's innate connection with things living, but not necessarily
immortal, is moving beyond words. But words are his forte, as this
example from 'Meiosis' shows.

'She claimed she remembered
the taste of her mother's milk
in her mouth, felt the midwife's
firm hand arranging her birth,
heard the creak of growing
embryonic bones in her head,
caught the whiff of her dad's
post-coital breath.'

In contrast, his understatement in looking back on the Troubles in
'Belfast,' is key. Many of us recall the terror of those times, but here is a
more oblique take on what could so easily happen again.

'It looks pristine,
the shattered paving stones replaced
with newly quarried pieces.
Underfoot, their piebald shadows
dapple into checkerboards of light
like some vast game
the children turn to hopscotch,
and what was there before the bomb
        is gone,
there's just the shadow's dance
across the sunlit street.'

This almost sideways look, rather than a rant, makes it all the more
powerful.

'Toybox' is another effective yet understated expression of memory and
the lingering symbolism of what it contains.

'In a box of forgotten things,
this year's spiders are busy
adding twelve months more
to thirty years of thin
embalming, silk.
No one knows they're there

and nobody remembers
all the toys and books
cocooned in 1986.'

However, the subject will remember them

'suspended in the matrix
of his memory
until his last breath blows
their cobwebbed carcasses away.'

Visual and again, empathic, without overload. Many of us have hoarded things which we must one day leave for ever…'

*

In my back-cover précis of *Heft* I wrote, 'Never mind the Book of Common Prayer, this collection should be gifted to everyone

'still falling through the fault lines
and other fontanelles
spinning like a penny
between heads and tails.'

At the end of this inspiring journey are the poet's Notes, adding yet more depth to his vision and explorations into what it means to be alive, and also to leave this mysterious, troubled but often inspiring world.

Sally Spedding

ovacome..
ovarian cancer charity

Ovarian cancer charity Ovacome is inviting short story submissions on the theme of "overcoming" for a contest it hopes will raise awareness of the disease and the work it does in supporting those affected by it.

The competition is open to all British residents. The theme can be interpreted in many different ways including overcoming fear, isolation, prejudice, setbacks – the possibilities are endless.

The judges are best-selling novelist, broadcaster, and author of *Eats, Shoots & Leaves*, Lynne Truss, crime writer and one-time music journalist William Shaw, and former BBC Travel Show presenter and writer Matthew Collins.

The competition will run from **July 31 to October 31**. Entrants must be aged 18-plus and pay £5 to submit their story. Enter at **www.ovacome.org.uk/Event/writing-competition**

Entries should be 2000 words or less and the winner, announced at the end of December, will be awarded £250

Ovacom wants to encourage entries from anyone who enjoys or wants to try out writing; not just those affected by ovarian cancer. Creative writing promotes happiness and mental wellbeing and this is a great opportunity to express oneself during difficult times.

INDEX

Other anthologies and collections available from Stairwell Books

For further information please contact rose@stairwellbooks.com
www.stairwellbooks.co.uk
@stairwellbooks